THREATENING DEMOCRACY

THREATENING DEMOCRACY
SLAPPs and the Judicial Repression
of Political Discourse

NORMAND LANDRY

Translated by
HOWARD SCOTT

Fernwood Publishing • Halifax & Winnipeg

Copyright © 2014 Normand Landry
Translation © 2014 Howard Scott
© Les Éditions Écosociété, 2012, for the original French edition
First published in 2012 by Les Éditions Écosociété, Montréal, under the title
SLAPP: *bâillonnement et répression judiciaire du discours politique,*

All rights reserved. No part of this book may be reproduced or transmitted in
any form by any means without permission in writing from the publisher,
except by a reviewer, who may quote brief passages in a review.

Text design: Brenda Conroy
Cover design: John van der Woude
Printed and bound in Canada by Hignell Book Printing

Published by Fernwood Publishing
32 Oceanvista Lane, Black Point, Nova Scotia, B0J 1B0
and 748 Broadway Avenue, Winnipeg, Manitoba, R3G 0X3
www.fernwoodpublishing.ca

Fernwood Publishing Company Limited gratefully acknowledges the financial support
of the Government of Canada through the Canada Book Fund and the Canada Council
for the Arts, the Nova Scotia Department of Communities, Culture and Heritage,
the Manitoba Department of Culture, Heritage and Tourism under the
Manitoba Publishers Marketing Assistance Program and the Province of Manitoba,
through the Book Publishing Tax Credit, for our publishing program.

Library and Archives Canada Cataloguing in Publication

Landry, Normand
[SLAPP. English]
Threatening democracy: SLAPPs and the judicial repression of political discourse /
Normand Landry; translator, Howard Scott.

Translation of: SLAPP.
Includes bibliographical references.
ISBN 978-1-55266-660-9 (pbk.)

1. Malicious prosecution. 2. Freedom of speech. 3. Political persecution.
I. Scott, Howard, 1952-, translator II. Title. III. Title: SLAPP. English.

K933.L3613 2014   346.03'34   C2014-900483-4

Contents

Introduction 7

1 What Is a SLAPP? 12
    Concepts and Definitions 13
    Summary 27

2 The Mechanisms and Processes of SLAPPs 30
    An Established Formula 32
    SLAPP, Law and Democracy: Fundamental Principles 43

3 Legal Intimidation and Legislation: International and National Perspectives . 53
    The United States on the Front Line 54
    The Australian Case 62
    The Canadian Case 67
    A Few Points of Analysis 79

4 Fighting SLAPPs: The Quebec Experience 87
    Getting SLAPPs Recognized 87
    The Écosociété Case and the
    Introduction of the First Anti-SLAPP Bill 93
    What Should Be Done? Lessons from the Quebec Experience 106
    Conclusion 112

5 SLAPPs as a Symptom 117
    The Judicialization of Public Debates 117
    Legal Inequality, Political Domination 124
    Mitigating the Symptoms 128

6 Conclusion 131

Appendices 136
    Appendix 1: Bill 9 136
    Appendix 2: British Columbia Bill (excerpts) 139
    Appendix 3: California Code of Civil Procedure 144

Bibliography 149

Introduction

Almost two centuries ago, Charles-Louis de Secondat, an enlightened nobleman better known as Baron de la Brède et de Montesquieu, declared wisely: "There is no greater tyranny than that which is perpetrated under the shield of the law and in the name of justice." Like many truths, this maxim has stood the test of time and remains a sad reality. The tyranny referred to by Montesquieu unfortunately endures, and is expressed insidiously, treacherously, with the tacit complicity of the institutions responsible for protecting the masses from the abuses of authoritarianism. Tyrants, great or small, know how to use the legal system shamelessly to crush their adversaries. It is no longer necessary to have them convicted, dragged to the scaffold or jailed. They simply trap them in the labyrinth of the contemporary legal system, an institution that has become a prison from which hapless defendants try to escape in vain. Because of its shortcomings, its slowness, the excessive costs that it generates, and through its very logic, the legal system itself becomes the punishment for those who oppose the tyrant in what has become a bitter irony.

This book offers an introduction to a phenomenon of legal intimidation that targets socially and politically active citizens. This phenomenon, addressed through the concept of the strategic lawsuit against public participation (SLAPP), implies a deliberate instrumentalization of legal proceedings as a weapon of intimidation, censorship and political reprisal in social and political conflicts. The image associated with this acronym suggests a violent shock: a person, group or community being "slapped." Evocatively titled books and scholarly articles dealing with this concept thus portray its violence: the strategy has been called a "slapp in the face of democracy" (Donson 2000), an action intended to "slapp resistance" (Rowell 1998), that requires the development of legislative countermeasures to give them "the knockout punch" (Corby 1998). In French, they are called *poursuites stratégiques contre la mobilisation publique*, or in Quebec, *poursuites-bâillons* (gag suits).[1]

Many have tried to fight this practice. In the United States, Europe, Australia and Canada, citizens, jurists, political representatives and academics have mobilized to get laws passed in order to curb the phenomenon. Such efforts have had mixed results. Some have been met with the rejection of legislators and jurists who did not see the need or relevance of legislating on the issue. Others have led to the adoption of rather ineffective laws that show a lack of political will to act forcefully on the issue. Some, finally, have led to the passage of stronger laws that now serve as models internationally. Moral victories can also, occasionally, be victories of substance.

The SLAPP phenomenon is difficult to quantify, although efforts have been made by some researchers (see Chapter 2). In the absence of archived legal decisions explicitly cataloguing SLAPP suits (which are rare when there are no provisions to combat them in the jurisdictions where they seem to be common) that can be consulted, it is difficult to find data other than anecdotal evidence on the presence and extent of the phenomenon in a given territory.

The frequent incredulity encountered among elected officials with regard to the need to act to curb the phenomenon is therefore understandable. The number of legal cases that have been called SLAPPs by Canadian courts remains all in all rather low. In addition, many SLAPP-like legal conflicts are settled out of court, and thus avoid being labelled as such by legal institutions. Legislators and the legal community therefore have difficulty measuring the phenomenon. Given the tendency to see SLAPP-like cases as isolated instances of abuse, they are hesitant to admit that there is a real problem of legal intimidation that would require legislative action. Michaelin Scott and Chris Tollefson provide an excellent analysis of the substantial problems encountered by those who attempt to define the phenomenon:

> SLAPPs are usually framed using a wide variety of tort claims including defamation, conspiracy, trespass, interference with contractual relations, inducing breach of contract and nuisance. Given that SLAPPs will often closely resemble an ordinary tort lawsuit, identifying SLAPPs can be difficult. These definitional difficulties also present challenges for those who seek to quantify the pervasiveness of the SLAPP phenomenon; including the frequency with which such suits have been filed, and the magnitude of their impact in terms of squandered public and private resources.
>
> Contributing to this quantification challenge is the fact that, much of the time, SLAPP cases do not proceed to trial. Given their limited resources, many targets are unable to mount a vigorous defence of their rights. As noted above, in many cases, victory over a potential SLAPP target is achieved without a suit being filed, with the mere threat of litigation dissuading the target from pursuing the battle any further. (Scott and Tollefson 2010: 46)

This situation enormously complicates the work of citizen groups calling for the adoption of anti-SLAPP legal measures. How can the severity of a phenomenon be proven when there are such significant methodological problems for those who wish to quantify it? Also, in the absence of formal recognition of the existence of the phenomenon by the judicial elites, how can anyone demonstrate that these are not isolated cases of abuse by an unscrupulous few individuals and businesses, but an established practice of legal intimidation targeting activists and politically engaged citizens?

Constructivist sociology teaches us that no social problem exists independently of the environments and actors that have generated and observed it. In other words, putting a social issue on the public agenda — the destruction of a fragile habitat, the social and economic marginalization of recent immigrants, urban violence — is essentially the outcome of a rhetorical contest between stakeholders with opposing positions on the question. This does not mean that certain (sometimes worrying) phenomena such as pollution, social exclusion and violence do not exist, but that to make them social problems — recognized as requiring action — it is necessary to express and interpret these phenomena as essentially negative situations requiring corrective measures. A society becomes aware of a social problem through a process of questioning, in which different actors struggle to define the issue's attributes and dimensions and, in a perhaps more significant way still, to identify those responsible, the causes and the possible remedies.

This rule applies equally to the anti-SLAPP struggle. Citizens who want to fight SLAPPs need to first of all strive to define the terms of the debate and the issues surrounding these suits. This means that they have to present a phenomenon or particular situation explicitly as a problem calling for collective action — and allocate duties and responsibilities to their various partners and interlocutors.[2]

This book represents a modest contribution to such efforts to frame SLAPPs as a scourge that needs to be identified, recognized and fought. The complex mechanisms of SLAPPs require detailed examination. As such, the book deals with the concept of the SLAPP, looks at its inherent conceptual problems, summarizes its associated social, political and psychological issues, and outlines the main rights and freedoms that it threatens. The book also discusses the processes by which politically active citizens are dragged out of the public space of political discussion and confined to the judicial space, outlines legal and political measures that have been taken at the national and international levels in order to fight against this phenomenon, and proposes a few concrete courses of action.

SLAPPs are most interesting — and revealing — when they are looked at as a symptom of a widespread judicial pathology rather than as an isolated problem. Although they represent a real and serious threat to our deliberative democracy, SLAPPs are but one symptom among many of much deeper problems eroding our legal system and infecting the social fabric. It is no surprise that such failures of justice, which people in legal circles have so much trouble defining, are resistant to the usual remedies proposed within the institution. These dysfunctions result from the capitalist relationships that have seeped into the liberal legal system. The commodification of legal representation services — as supposedly inevitable and natural — is at the heart of the problem. Processes of judicial inflation and densification (the perpetual growth of the domains regulated by law and the increasing complexity of legal rules) are also to blame.[3] In philosophy and the social sciences, the increasing influence on social life of the law and associated bureaucratic processes is interpreted as the bureaucratic colonization of the lifeworld — a free, self-regulating and spontaneous space of encounters and discussion that contribute to the organization of society (see Habermas 1984 and 1996).

My relationship with this subject is very intimate. I studied strategic lawsuits against public participation as the subject of a doctoral thesis. This book is intended to provide a simplified synthesis of this work, of what has been an obsession of mine for more than four years. But also, and above all, this book, like the thesis that preceded it, is largely the product of encounters: encounters with ordinary citizens who have neither grand-sounding titles that give them any particular authority or significant political influence, and even less the financial resources and economic affluence that would make it easy for them to get involved in public life. These men and women have taken it upon themselves to act and talk, to question and protest, and to oppose those more powerful than themselves. And they did this in the public interest and in accordance with their individual consciences and ethics. For their audacity, they have been severely punished. As brave as they were, these people have been sorely tested through the slow agony of judicial entanglements. Some have suffered from depression; others have left the country. All have experienced considerable stress and many of them will never be properly compensated for the harm they have suffered. Their fates have varied: some have reluctantly signed out-of-court settlements to free themselves from the judicial maze; many, the less fortunate, have remained entangled interminably. In the face of the giants they were opposing and their batteries of lawyers, others have had no choice but to declare bankruptcy and to go on to something else, disengage from public life. Who could blame them? The decision to abandon the fight, though it may bring psychological relief, is morally painful. This judicial form of punishment, reserved for those who publicly oppose adversaries — adversaries who can afford the luxury of legal representation — had to be named and exposed.

Following similar experiences that had occurred previously in other countries, a Quebec anti-SLAPP movement emerged during the five years preceding the publication of the first French edition of this book (SLAPP: *bâillonnement et répression judiciaire du discours politique*, Les Éditions Écosociété, 2012), which served to define and put a label on a revolting practice of legal intimidation. This practice, based on the political cooptation of the bias in the judiciary in favour of the classes and categories of actors who possess the capital required for legal representation, has thus been exposed to the light of day. Those being punished by the legal system had a right to speak; their stories have generated vast amounts of empathy in the population — probably because these men and women, anonymous as they were, were a reflection of a population that saw itself collectively as victims of this practice. Anti-SLAPP efforts in Quebec brought results and led to the adoption by the National Assembly of a law called *An Act to amend the Code of Civil Procedure to prevent improper use of the courts and promote freedom of expression and citizen participation in public debate*, a title that leaves few doubts as to its laudable objectives. Quebec thus became the second Canadian province to adopt anti-SLAPP legislation and, for the time being at least, it is the only jurisdiction in the country that has such a law in effect.[4]

The essential question now in Quebec is to determine to what extent this legislation will be capable of fulfilling its mandate. The first cases suggest relatively satisfactory outcomes, although in some respects concerns remain: the legislative model adopted in Quebec is far from perfect. Yet, in English Canada, the fundamental question remains of how to get similar measures adopted by provincial political elites who have so far been resistant to any meaningful legislative action against SLAPPs. This book, in bearing witness to citizen efforts to protect political speech and gain a foothold in the context of Quebec, is based on the hope that the Quebec experience will serve as an inspiration for similar mobilization efforts across Canada and abroad.

Chamfort said: "The justice of men is always a form of power." Reflections on SLAPPs call into question the expansion of judicial power, and thus offer a key avenue to a broader critical discussion on our legal system, its dysfunctions and how it interferes in our political and democratic life.

Notes

1. The choice in French of the word "mobilisation" rather than "participation" may seem incongruous. In fact, the English term seems to me to put a slight emphasis on the idea of a legitimate, ordinary, often individual action, while the French term better suggests joint actions. See MacDonald et al. 2007.
2. The question of strategic lawsuits against public participation has, for example, been closely associated with the concept of freedom of expression in Quebec. The high regard — at once legal, political and social — that this normative principle enjoys in the province enables anti-SLAPP activists to demand accountability in both political and legal spheres. Quebec legislators were therefore called upon to make this a priority, since the Quebec government has been reminded by citizen groups of its responsibility to protect freedom of expression.
3. These elements are presented and detailed in Chapter 5.
4. British Columbia, the first province to adopt such legislation, soon repealed it in 2001 after there was a change in government, much to the consternation of the civil society groups that had fought for its adoption.

Chapter 1

What Is a SLAPP?

The story, sadly, is all too typical. A bailiff rings your doorbell. You get a "slapp" in the face through an intermediary. You're given a letter demanding hundreds of thousands or even millions of dollars. Your crime — because, as you read the application instituting proceedings, it becomes apparent that you are considered to be, at best, a reckless and irresponsible individual, at worst a criminal — is to have spoken out. To have acted, to have denounced. This is obviously not explained in so many words in the documents that have been transmitted to you. Instead they speak of conspiracy, defamation, interference with business and contractual relations or some other obscure and confusing pretext of the kind. The tone used is aggressive; the jargon in which the document is written makes you feel helpless. That feeling of distress will only grow with time, as the lawyer's bills and legal procedures pile up. Faced with such a threat, with the risk of losing everything, the immediate reflex, the most natural one, is to disengage. Stop everything. Keep quiet. Salvage something, save your own skin. They already have you where they want you. You've been gagged. And this is all happening with the implicit complicity of a legal system now acting as a tool of censorship.

This in itself is hard enough to deal with. Even more difficult is the realization that a threat is now hanging over the heads of your loved ones, your family, your colleagues and friends. Life savings, plans for the future, the countless hours devoted to your defence, the people who counted on you to lead the struggle you believed in: all this swallowed up in a unjustified and unnecessary legal battle that causes the total disruption of your life.

Perhaps you won't react this way. Perhaps you'll be furious, galvanized by the outrageous nature of the whole business. If you make the choice to continue the political struggle, to fight this attempt at legal intimidation, you will certainly have to also fight your lawyer (because you'll need one, and a good one), who will advise, to no great surprise, caution and restraint. He or she will probably encourage you to withdraw from the cause you were active in. By doing so, your own lawyer will unintentionally become the accomplice of your adversary. Both will make every effort to keep you quiet, docile and isolated. Their objectives will differ, of course, but the result will be the same: silence, your silence. And so the muzzling of a victim of a strategic lawsuit against public participation is achieved.

What should be done? The first step is to get to know the nature of the evil. To do this, it has to be defined correctly.

Concepts and Definitions

Once "slapped," the first thing the victim of a strategic lawsuit against public participation has to do is understand the nature of the process that has been initiated against him or her. The phenomenon, as disturbing, widespread and problematic as it is, is still largely unknown to the general public.

Much, however, has been accomplished in recent decades to increase awareness in the population (as well as in the legal and political communities) about the problems and issues associated with SLAPPs. Recognition of the existence of such a strategy of legal intimidation specifically targeting citizens taking part in public debates came first in the United States. Then it gradually spread, although in a more limited way, to other Western countries — with Canada, Australia, the United Kingdom and France experiencing similar phenomena.

The social and political issues raised by this kind of lawsuit are easy to identify. However, defining the phenomenon and suggesting concrete solutions turns out to be more problematic. What are the characteristics of SLAPPs? How can we know, how can we dare to claim that we are faced with — or are victims of — the phenomenon? A diagnostic definition is required.

By strategic lawsuits against public participation, I mean lawsuits that have been: 1) initiated in response to citizen mobilization or expression with respect to an issue of public interest; 2) with the intention of instrumentalizing the legal process; 3) in order to limit the scope of the freedom of expression of those individuals or organizations, to neutralize their actions or to limit, restrict or put an end to discussion and public mobilization with respect to the initial issue under dispute; 4) by using the courts for purposes of intimidation, coercion or political reprisal.[1]

This definition includes a few thorny elements that will require explanation and clarification. Note the emphasis on the *strategic* nature of the lawsuit. This necessarily implies an intentional and deliberate action by the instigator. It is therefore a legal undertaking that is based not on the law — in order to, in good faith, remedy damage suffered — but on the abusive instrumentalization of the legal process in order to limit, prevent or punish public mobilization. Two key characteristics delimit what is meant by strategic lawsuit against public participation: it is 1) a deliberate attempt at legal intimidation; 2) with objectives that are essentially political or economic. For Professor Penelope Canan (whose works, published in collaboration with her colleague George W. Pring, originated the term (Pring and Canan 1996)), the motifs and objectives behind this kind of lawsuits are essentially of four types:

1. Punish social opposition that has succeeded in making its voice heard on an issue of public interest;
2. Forestall future social opposition on issues of public policy;
3. Intimidate opposing parties; and

4. Mobilize the legal system as an additional arena that can be instrumentalized to win a political or economic battle. (Canan 1989: 30)

The reference to damages suffered is therefore only a pretext for a process intended to lead to an impoverishment of public mobilization. This does not, however, mean that it is a pure fabrication. The plaintiff can very well instrumentalize a legal fault committed in relationship to a criticism or a public opposition to its activities or projects in order to muzzle political adversaries. The judicial confinement of those adversaries permits the plaintiff to regain an initiative that it had lost in the public sphere. The damage suffered gives the legal undertaking an appearance of legitimacy that assures its effectiveness. It is consequently wrong to believe, contrary to what is sometimes claimed in the socio-legal literature, that SLAPPs have absolutely no foundation and that there is necessarily an absence of legal fault on the part of the parties targeted by them.[2]

SLAPPs thus conceal intentions *other* than obtaining a victory on legal substance — something that is often extremely difficult to obtain in a courtroom, even when the cases presented are well prepared.[3] These intentions are essentially political: the goal is to weaken social criticism in order to impose one's will in a public arena and stifle the efforts of adversaries who are hindering the realization of specific ideas and plans. The legal action is based on an evaluation of the imbalance of the strengths and financial means of adversaries. The party that has initiated the proceedings — the SLAPPer — seeks to convert that imbalance into a tool of censorship. This is achieved very simply, through the forced absorption of the private capital of the defendants in a legal dispute for which they have little or no capacity to bear the costs.

The judicial machinery then drains the financial, human and time resources of the SLAPP victims over a long period of time. This extremely effective process diverts the adversaries from their political actions and pushes communities into passivity and docility. The monetary damages claimed by the SLAPPer — frequently disproportionate to the fault of which it claims to be a victim and to the capacity of its adversaries to pay — have a dissuasive effect, like a sword of Damocles that threatens to fall on anyone who dares oppose its plans.

The strategic nature of SLAPPs thus supposes a deliberate instrumentalization of the legal apparatus to suppress citizen participation in public debate. In this way, it becomes a direct threat to what some call the integrity of the legal system. The fault committed by the instigator of the SLAPP is thus two-fold: it is not only a violation of the fundamental rights of the opposing party, but also a diversion from the goals of the legal system (to ensure justice), which has serious social and political consequences. This two-fold fault explains why, when it is recognized that parties have sued their adversaries improperly, they are sometimes obliged to pay substantial punitive and exemplary damages.[4]

Therefore lawsuits that have the consequence, but not the objective, of muzzling or punishing political adversaries cannot be qualified as SLAPPs. They are something else (as we will see shortly). Similarly, the legal proceedings undertaken following private disputes between parties, without public or political dimensions, should not be associated with this concept. Trade disputes and private disagreements between citizens do not have direct negative effects on the conduct of public debate.

The question of intentions is therefore central to the concept of strategic lawsuits against public participation. However, while the determination of the intentions of the parties initiating the proceedings is essential to understanding the phenomenon, it causes huge headaches for those who want to curb it. The question is as follows: how can a court be quickly convinced that the case before it manifests a deliberate attempt to muzzle or repress legitimate citizen opposition? In the absence of such a demonstration, and in the jurisdictions where there are no measures to quickly quash legal proceedings that interfere with the defendant's public participation, it is more than likely that the court will refuse to promptly dismiss the proceedings. It will instead consider it legitimate to prolong the ordeal of the victims of judicial abuse.

SLAPPs are abusive legal actions undertaken following citizen participation in public debate. The context of the legal conflict is therefore an essential component of this type of suit: it is closely — and strictly — associated with a controversy on an issue of public interest. It therefore calls into question a certain number of elements presented in Table 1.

SLAPPs give undue political advantage to their instigators and favour their interests to the detriment of a group or community that is diverted from its projects, ideas or actions. They are attempts, in other words, to circumvent the deliberative

Table 1

Constitutive elements of the issue				
Precedence given to private interests over the public interest during political controversies	Impacts on public mobilization	Organization of power relationships between the various spheres of our societies	Citizen participation in the discussion of public affairs and in democratic governance	Organization of the rights and duties of the parties in the conduct of political disputes
Details on what is at stake				
Instrumentalization of judicial procedures and processes in order to punish adversaries and defeat resistance and opposition in the public arena	The psychological and financial collapse of the victims, their confinement inside the legal system, the weakening or cessation of political activities	Translation of economic inequalities into judicial inequality for the benefit of more wealthy individuals and groups	Fear, excessive caution, refusal to get involved in public debates observed among victims or witnesses	Balance of the rights, duties and responsibilities participants in public debates; interference and intrusion of the legal (the law) and the judicial (processes associated with the conduct of legal disputes) in the democratic life of a community

processes inherent to political disputes. Is there a factory releasing noxious gases and poisoning the residents in its vicinity? A SLAPP will temper their passion for publicly demanding that the company comply with existing regulations. Does a promoter want to build a huge recreational complex in a quiet neighbourhood? The citizen voices raised against the project will be reduced to a whisper after a legal "slapp" has been given to a few carefully chosen individuals. The entrepreneurs and industrialists who claimed they have the right to freely sue (and this is profoundly contradictory) show a deep distrust for a free market of ideas where the value of the proposals being debated prevail in the face of the financial or political power of the parties involved.

SLAPPs are aimed at creating among their victims and the population in general a reflex of self-censorship and excessive caution that stifles public mobilization. The fear generated by lawsuits works to discipline those who share the convictions or political activities of targeted parties. It pressures them to be silent and to retreat, since the fear of seeing themselves dragged in turn before the courts usually spreads to the powerless witnesses of the collapse of the parties who have been "slapped." This is perhaps the most pernicious aspect of a SLAPP: like a stone dropped into a pool of water, it produces shockwaves that go far beyond the inner circle of its victims. A whole group of people, a whole community is muzzled by fear. The SLAPP victim serves as an example to the population, a clear warning: legal entanglements await anyone who might be foolish enough to follow this person into the public arena. The punishment is manifested in a family that is forced to re-mortgage its house and who watches, powerlessly, as its savings quickly evaporate. It is also illustrated through depression, loss of employment or the frequent disintegration of social bonds that the victims previously had with other members of their communities. The effect of the lawsuit can last for a long time, spreading its poison outward through its victims.

This kind of lawsuit generates what is called a "chilling effect" on public mobilization. SLAPPs thus jeopardize the mechanisms through which public opinion can be expressed and become a distinct political force. The danger is that they can permit a certain category of actors to impose themselves politically in social and political conflicts through the legal muzzling of opposing parties; they render the legal process an additional political lever available to a specific class, which possesses extensive legal capital and proportional financial means, in order to crush social and political dissidence. SLAPPs thus constitute a direct threat to the legal system, which they blithely discredit and exploit.

Serge Galipeau and Christine Landry live in the municipality of Cantley, in the Ottawa Valley. Like their fellow citizens, they lived through many years of significant environmental safety problems, caused, according to the local residents, by the gas emissions from a dry materials dump located nearby. Over the years, around twenty investigations were carried out on the site and dozens of offence notices were issued against its owners. Many families, close to 200 individuals,

> We had to re-mortgage our house, which was almost paid for, to pay the lawyer's fees, but also all the costs of building our defence, access to information, photocopies, briefs; it went on and on....
>
> How do you protect yourself against SLAPPs? It is very, very simple: you say nothing, you write nothing, you comment on nothing, you play dead. Then you won't have any more SLAPPs. (Galipeau 2008)

were also evacuated in March 2005 when an underground fire started on the site causing toxic gas emissions (see Bourgault-Côté 2007).

The owners of the dump always denied the allegations about the operation of the site being connected to the environmental health problems of the citizens in the region and used various legal remedies against their opponents over the years. Serge Galipeau and Christine Landry, who were very active in the citizen movement asking for the closure of the landfill, were severely affected by these proceedings. In August 2006, they were sued for $750,000 by their adversaries, later increased to 1.25 million dollars.[5]

The legal action taken against these citizens generated extensive media coverage and were referred to, both by those citizens and by various commentators in civil society and the media, as a strategic lawsuit against public participation (see Santerre 2008 and Société Radio-Canada 2008, February 18). In spite of the consensus among various municipalities and government authorities about the environmental and public health issues associated with the dry materials dump in Cantley,[6] the lawsuit against Serge Galipeau and Christine Landry remained active for many years. Alone, they had to assume the costs for their defence and invested more than 4,300 hours in preparing their case. This tenacity eventually brought results.

Serge Galipeau and Christine Landry got the defamation lawsuit against them thrown out after four years of legal proceedings. The court agreed in July 2010 that "at first glance, the lawsuit instituted by the plaintiffs against the petitioners has all

> After fighting for 20 months against the gas emissions, they faced the enormous stress of the lawsuit. Anxiety, loss of sleep, severe stress.... Every day, for the past 18 months, the last thought we have when we go to bed at night is the lawsuit, then the first thought we have when we get up in the morning is the lawsuit, then every hour of the day, I think at least once of the lawsuit. Our quality of life is completely destroyed....
>
> The impact on the social community and the neighbours of the site? Well, they're afraid of getting the same kind of lawsuit as us, so they keep quiet. Ninety per cent of the people who were on the committee stopped talking, no longer complained, it was over. (Assemblée Nationale du Québec 2008)

the appearances of a SLAPP suit."⁷ Forty-eight months of legal proceedings were required for a court to reach that conclusion. Judge Pierre Dallaire subsequently recognized the role played by Serge Galipeau and Christine Landry — who had become standard bearers for the anti-SLAPP fight in Quebec — in putting abusive lawsuits on the public agenda, and he sentenced the plaintiffs to pay them $142,535.86 in damages and punitive damages.⁸ In spite of this judgment, it is unlikely that Galipeau and Landry will receive the money awarded in damages, since the parties found at fault have declared bankruptcy or are subject to recovery action.⁹

Emergence and Various Uses of the Concept of SLAPPs

The first important studies on strategic lawsuits against public participation were carried out in the 1980s by Professors George W. Pring and Penelope Canan, then both working at the University of Denver. These pioneers endeavoured to define the strategic lawsuit against public participation according to one "primary" (essential) criterion and three secondary criteria. To be considered SLAPPs, suits had to, according to them:

1. Involve communications made to influence a government action or outcome;
2. Result in civil lawsuits (complaints, counterclaims, or cross-claims);
3. Be filed against nongovernment individuals or groups on;
4. A substantive issue of some public interest or social significance. (Pring and Canan 1996: 8)

More than twenty-five years after the publication of this first research, SLAPPs remain essentially understood in the United States as an illegitimate, abusive legal response to the exercise of the right to petition of American citizens. The right to petition includes among other things the right to address a complaint, to ask for assistance or to inform authorities about an issue, a problem or an opinion without fear of reprisals from the agents of the government or private actors. This right has been the subject of extensive interpretation in the United States, supported by jurisprudence that has significantly expanded the framework of legal protection offered to it.¹⁰ SLAPPs are considered to be a direct threat to American representative democracy because they weaken and corrupt the channels of communication between the representatives and the represented. These lawsuits have also been seen as serious attacks on the integrity of the American legal system, since SLAPPers have effectively converted judicial proceedings into a weapon of legal repression to discourage citizen participation in public debate.

The definition proposed by Pring and Canan is limited to communications addressed to authorities (which is extremely restrictive): it further involves a right to petition not necessarily found in other countries. This right, fundamental on American soil, is absent from the Canadian constitutional structure.¹¹ It would therefore be counterproductive, in Canada and Quebec, to think of the issue of strategic lawsuits against public participation in terms of the right to petition. More generally, since the law and legal culture vary from one society to another, it is difficult to import a legal definition verbatim. The concept of strategic lawsuit against public participation has also, in particular, been the subject of many definitions since the appearance of the concept in recent decades; some of these are outlined in Table 2.

Table 2

Authors/ judgments	Definitions (excerpts)	Key characteristics
Abell, David J.	First, SLAPP suits are frivolous civil actions that disguise constitutionally protected political activity as common tort claims. Second, the tort claims most frequently alleged by SLAPP plaintiffs include one or more of the following: defamation, interference with prospective advantage, interference with contractual relations, malicious prosecution, abuse of process, denial of Fifth or Fourteenth Amendment property rights, civil conspiracy, or nuisance. Third, the damages claimed are enormous relative to the resources of the defendant. Fourth, an individual defendant in a SLAPP suit is forced to incur considerable litigation costs, often resulting in the forced termination of the petitioning activity and the correspondent dropping of the suits (Abell 1993).	• SLAPP suits are frivolous legal actions attacking constitutionally protected political activities disguised as tort claims; • They usually allege of range of recurrent and relatively circumscribed offences; • The damages claimed are disproportionate in comparison with the defendant's resources; • The individuals targeted by SLAPPs have to assume significant legal costs. These costs pressure defendants petitioning public authorities to suspend their activities.
Barker, John C.	Strategic Lawsuits Against Public Participation, or "SLAPP suits" as they have become known, are defined as civil lawsuits filed with the dual intention of punishing those who have exercised their political rights under the Constitution and discouraging the same from engaging in similar conduct in the future (Barker 2004).	• SLAPPS are civil lawsuits with essentially two objectives: - Punish adversaries who have exercised their constitutional rights; - Discourage subsequent public mobilization.
Lott, Susan	SLAPPS are an explicitly political use of defamation and other tort actions for political or economic purposes.... The key aspect of the SLAPP, to force individuals into costly litigation, suggests that overall success of a SLAPP does not necessarily require a legal victory but a political one: to intimidate and to suppress criticism (Lott 2004).	• SLAPPS suppose the instrumentalization of the law for purposes other than obtaining a victory on substance; • They are based on forcing adversaries into a costly legal arena; • The action is effective when it intimidates adversaries and reduces them silence.

MacDonald, Roderick A., Daniel Jutras & Pierre Noreau	They are, essentially, 1) lawsuits 2) initiated against organizations or individuals 3) involved in the public arena within the framework of debates around collective issues, 4) and aimed at limiting the scope of freedom of expression of these organizations or individuals and to neutralize their action 5) by using the courts to intimidate them, impoverish them and divert them from their action (MacDonald et al. 2007).	• SLAPPs target citizens participating in public debate on issues of public interest; • They seek to restrict the freedom of expression of political opponents or to neutralize them; • The use of the courts makes it possible to intimidate, impoverish and divert activists from their political activities.
McBride, Edward W., Jr.	Strategic Lawsuits Against Public Participation ("SLAPPS") are a potent means of retaliating against individuals and groups who have petitioned the government on issues of public concern. SLAPPs are lawsuits instituted to intimidate political opponents by calling upon the courts to sanction constitutionally protected behaviour. Litigation is used to transfer a public debate from the political arena to the judicial arena, where the forum appears more favourable (McBride 1993).	• SLAPPs carry out reprisals against those who have previously petitioned the government on a question of public interest; • They appear as a mechanism for intimidation mobilizing the courts to sanction political activities protected by the constitution; • The lawsuit seeks to transfer a public debate taking place in a political arena to a judicial arena that is more favourable to the plaintiff.
Wilcox v. Superior Court (1994) [27 Cal. App. 4th 809]	SLAPP suits are brought to obtain economic advantage over the defendant, not to vindicate a legally recognizable right of the plaintiff. Indeed, one of the common characteristics of a SLAPP suit is its lack of merit. But lack of merit is not of concern to the plaintiff because the plaintiff does not expect to succeed in the lawsuit, only to tie up the defendant's resources for a sufficient length of time to accomplish plaintiff's underlying objective (Wilcox v. Superior Court, 27 Cal. App. 4th 809, 1994).	• The legal action seeks to instrumentalize an economic imbalance between adversaries; • SLAPPs are characterized by the lack of merit of the case; • The lawsuits seek to drain the resources of the adversary; • The lawsuit conceals an extralegal objective other than success on substance, a result not anticipated by the initiator of the action.

We quickly see emerge points of convergence among these definitions. First of all, the question of intentions seems to be paramount. SLAPPs conceal essentially political objectives — to intimidate adversaries, impose certain views in a public arena, repress actions and behaviours — by reframing them as legal objectives that could be legitimate: to obtain compensation and justice, set the record straight. Second, SLAPPs are intended to instrumentalize legal proceedings as a tool of social demobilization or legal repression: they use the rules governing legal disputes to undermine the exercise of fundamental rights protected by a legal system that is now the accomplice in their repressive function.

A Few Conceptual and Legal Problems

The legislative mechanisms adopted in various foreign jurisdictions in order to counteract strategic lawsuits against public participation are essentially of two types: there are those that protect, in essence, citizen mobilization and participation in public debate against the judicialization of social and political conflicts, and those, more limited, that are restricted only to abusive proceedings. The former gives qualified privilege to participants in public debate, as long as their actions are relevant and undertaken in good faith and in the public interest; these are aimed at the quick dismissal of civil proceedings that interfere with their activities. The latter propose mechanisms that make it easier to unmask and punish improper lawsuits,[12] while permitting suits that, although they could seriously affect the conduct of public debate, would not be considered abusive in a strictly legal sense. The central problem, from this point of view, is to establish mechanisms to quickly separate the good grain from the chaff, that is, to equip the courts so that they are better able to identify proceedings that conceal improper political intentions or the abusive use of legal proceedings.

Two cultures, two basic principles: while the former approach promotes full participation in public debate and tolerates to a certain extent the excesses and faults in law that sometimes result from this, the latter advocates individual responsibility and the balance of rights between "private" adversaries in the public arena. This distinction is important and results in significant problems of definition. For some, a SLAPP is a lawsuit that has the *effect* of limiting or restricting public mobilization of citizens — this is the approach often taken by American anti-SLAPP legislation. For others, a strategic lawsuit against public participation is a legal proceeding *intended* to limit or restrict the public mobilization of political adversaries.

The adoption of a particular approach by legislators who want to fight SLAPPs is a matter of political will as well as of legal and political culture. This being said, the difficulties — frequently substantial — of imposing on the defendant the burden of demonstrating the malicious nature of the plaintiff's intentions have led some authors to call for the abandonment of the criterion of intentionality associated with SLAPPs. This argument is made by Pamela Shapiro, for example:

> SLAPPs are a problem because of their effect on public speech, and not principally due to the SLAPP plaintiff's intention. While it is common to say that the SLAPP plaintiff sues specifically to prevent the interested party from intervening further, and the inclusion of the word *strategic* encourages this belief, it is more relevant that the lawsuits are often unfounded and that they have the *effect* rather than the aim of silencing the intervener. As such, although the catchy acronym has perhaps garnered SLAPPs more attention, the inclusion of the word "strategic" may be less than ideal. The acronym "LAPP," for Lawsuit *Affecting* Public Participation, may have been more accurate, if not quite as catchy. (Shapiro 2010: 16)

This is a key issue for public policy. Different legislative models that have been adopted or considered in Canada have asked defendants who consider themselves to be victims of SLAPPs to demonstrate before the court either that there are *probabilities* of improper intentions on the part of the plaintiff, or that there is a *realistic possibility* of the existence of such intentions.[13] These provisions impose an additional burden on the defendant, who has to not only prepare a defence, but also demonstrate a probability or a possibility of improper intentions on the part of their adversaries before the court — a task that could prove to be exhausting. What Shapiro proposes, and what certain American laws have established,[14] is the adoption of mechanisms permitting the dismissal of lawsuits that interfere with the public participation of the defendants, *whatever the intentions of the plaintiffs*. The defendants would therefore only have to demonstrate legitimate public participation to have the resulting lawsuit quashed. Their burden of proof would thus be considerably reduced, making dismissal of the suit — and, where applicable, the penalization of the party that initiated proceedings — much easier.

If, according to Shapiro (and others before her), the primary objective of effective anti-SLAPP legislation is not to acknowledge the abusive nature of the plaintiff's intentions but to protect freedom of expression, then why should this criterion of intentionality be maintained? This aspect of the discussion raises significant conceptual and legal issues.

As we have seen, the strategic nature of SLAPPs assumes a deliberate instrumentalization of the legal apparatus to stifle citizen participation in public debate. They permit a certain category of actors possessing extensive legal capital to impose themselves politically in social and political conflicts through the legal muzzling of opposing parties; they make the legal process an additional political lever available to economically advantaged individuals, classes and social groups in order to crush social and political dissidence. The outrageous nature of SLAPPs arises precisely from this principle of the conversion of economic inequalities into legal inequality as a means of political censorship.

The elimination of the criterion of intentionality would have the consequence of making irrelevant the question of the objectives of the party instigating proceedings that limit, restrict or prevent the free expression of citizens. It would thus deprive us of a necessary discussion on the role and the place occupied by legal intimidation in the weakening of processes through which citizens participate in public debate. It would be wrong to believe that all lawsuits that emerge from public debates are intended to be abusive or improper. While protection should be provided for those who get involve in public affairs from legal pitfalls associated with their political activities, it is important not to confuse legal actions undertaken in good faith, with the objective of remedying real or supposed damages, with proceedings that politically instrumentalize judicial proceedings. Errors, faults and irregularities that require action by the courts can be committed on any side during public debates. The question is whether participants in public debate should be made responsible — that is, should they have to answer for their actions and words before the courts — or else should we refuse to allow private conflicts arising from public controversies to become legal disputes.

Some legislation adopted or considered internationally has followed the second approach. It asks the courts to refuse to hear or dismiss cases that appear to be interfering with the fundamental political rights of the parties involved. This is a way of preventing the legal system from interfering with political debate. SLAPPs are not, however, solely problematic because they constitute a sanitizing phenomenon of interference by the legal sphere in political debate[15]; they also constitute a major social and political issue because they reflect the political cooptation of legal proceedings initiated to crush or repress speech and actions related to issues of public interest.

Eliminating the criterion of intentionality thus tends to obscure, rather than clarify, our understanding of the phenomenon — and consequently limits the capacity to act appropriately to deal with it. How then does this dilemma get resolved? On the one hand, relinquishing the criterion of intentionality impairs an understanding of one of the SLAPP's basic dimensions: it is an attempt at legal intimidation that should be severely repressed and not a simple (although highly problematic) judicialization of a private dispute resulting from opposing interests and perspectives in the public arena. On the other hand, maintaining this criterion greatly complicates the implementation of effective legal solutions that could be adopted legislatively, since the courts usually refuse to quickly dismiss proceedings that do not immediately appear improper. The solution to this problem consists in a more refined analysis that adopts a new, broader concept of the "gag suit"(translated from the French word "*poursuite-bâillon*"), which coexists with the concept of the strategic lawsuit against public participation.

Gag Suit and SLAPPs

The expressions "strategic lawsuit against public participation" and "gag suit" are frequently used in Quebec as synonyms (see, for example, MacDonald et al. 2007). This is a mistake. It is more appropriate analytically to differentiate "strategic lawsuit against public participation" from "gag suit." This distinction is important and leads to differing interpretations of the problems created by the mobilization of the legal system during social and political controversies.

Let us start by defining the term. "Gag suits" are lawsuits that have been: 1) initiated in response to citizen mobilization or expression with respect to an issue of public interest; 2) with the effect of limiting the scope of or halting public participation of the parties targeted by the legal proceedings instigated against them or to weaken, restrict or stop public discussion and mobilization on the initial issue under dispute.

A gag suit is a procedure that judicializes and privatizes a conflict occurring in the public arena. In doing so, it interferes with the public debate and the exercise of the political rights of actors targeted. It thus produces social effects analogous to those of SLAPPs: it confines actors active in the public sphere to the legal arena, intimidates communities and reframes the nature of disputes according to essentially private perspectives. It is not abusive in the sense that it is assumed that the gag suit does not conceal intentions of intimidation or legal repression; such suits should, however, be quickly dismissed by the courts because of the effects that they have on public debate and on the groups they target. Gag suits can be identified by their *effects*: SLAPPs can be recognized both by the *intentions* of the party instigating the proceedings, the *nature* of the legal proceedings used and their *impacts* on the individuals and groups that they target.

Table 3 should help us to differentiate these concepts. On the one hand, SLAPPs are essentially attempts at legal intimidation, while gag suits constitute a phenomenon of sanitizing public debate through the use of the courts in order to obtain compensation for (real or presumed) damages incurred by private individuals during public controversies and debates.[16] The objectives of the two processes also differ: the political (and abusive) objectives of SLAPPs contrast the supposedly legal

Table 3

Definitions	Main elements of definition	General objectives of the legal mechanisms that are supposed to counteract the phenomenon
Strategic lawsuits against public participation: lawsuits with the following characteristics: 1) initiated in response to citizen mobilization or expression with respect to an issue of public interest, 2) with the intention of instrumentalizing the legal process, 3) in order to limit the scope of the freedom of expression of those individuals or organizations, to neutralize their actions or to limit, restrict or put an end to discussion and public mobilization with respect to the initial issue under dispute, 4) by using the courts for purposes of intimidation, coercion or political reprisal.	• **Procedure**: deliberate instrumentalization of the judicial process in order to force costs and legal proceedings on adversaries; • **Target:** action against individuals and groups that have participated or are participating in a debate of public interest; • **Objectives:** essentially political in nature: crush dissidence, intimidate opponents, repress political actions; • **Impacts:** legal intimidation, social demobilization, diversion of the legal system.	• **Protect** citizens and organizations against court action that limits their freedom of expression or their right to public participation; • **Compensate** citizens and groups that have incurred costs; • **Dissuade** potential SLAPPers from misusing legal proceedings; • **Punish** those who use this strategy.
Gag suits: lawsuits with the following characteristics: 1) initiated in response to citizen mobilization or expression with respect to an issue of public interest, 2) and have the effect of limiting the scope of or halting public participation of the parties targeted by the legal proceedings instigated against them or to weaken, restrict or stop public discussion and mobilization on the initial issue under dispute.	• **Procedure:** reference by the plaintiff to real or supposed damages in relationship to a public debate that has the effect of forcing costs and legal proceedings on the parties targeted; • **Target:** action against individuals and groups that have participated or are participating in a debate of public interest; • **Objectives:** legal objectives: obtain compensation and justice; • **Impacts:** legal intimidation, social demobilization.	• **Reject** the judicialization of private disputes resulting from participation in public debate; • **Protect** citizens and organizations against court action that limits their freedom of expression or their right to public participation; • **Compensate** citizens and groups that have incurred legal costs.

objectives of gag suits. Both raise the spectre of an undue judicialization of public debates, with SLAPPs adding in particular a principle of diversion and improper political cooptation of the legal system. This conceptual clarification will permit us to establish the foundations for a mechanism to protect those participating in public debate from an excessive judicialization of political disputes, reprimand SLAPPs and avoid entanglements of defendants in proceedings aimed at demonstrating the improper aims of those suing them.

On this particular aspect, Shapiro is absolutely correct: the basic challenge is to protect the capacity of citizens to participate in public debate and express themselves without fear of onerous lawsuits. It is important therefore, first and foremost, to ensure the prompt rejection of such suits, and then to penalize the instigators of abusive legal proceedings. The most appropriate method to accomplish this would have two stages[17]:

> For present purposes it is perhaps desirable to create a means for summary dismissal based upon unjustifiable interference with the right to public participation rather than improper purpose, but to also create a separate cause of action in which an individual sued for the purpose of silencing or punishing public participation can seek punitive and exemplary damages. (Bover and Parnell 2001)

This would mean, first of all, the adoption of provisions permitting the courts to dismiss, both quickly and effectively, lawsuits brought against citizens or organizations who have participated in good faith in public debate. Participants in public debate should thus be granted qualified privilege for related actions, gestures and communications. In the absence of bad faith (which must be demonstrated by the party instigating the proceedings), the proceedings should be dismissed by a court, which would refuse to permit the judicialization of the dispute between the parties to interfere with continuation of the public debate. The objective of this approach is to counteract the harmful social and political effects of gag suits.

Then, and if it appears to the court that the lawsuit instigated against the citizens or organizations was abusive in the sense that it was aimed at intimidation or repression of a social or political participation, the instigators of the action — including the legal experts that conducted the proceedings — should be severely punished. This should be done through the adoption of specific measures favouring unmasking the abusive nature of the legal proceedings undertaken. This punishment can only occur if the court rules on the abusive nature of the proceedings instigated against the defendant: in other words, the court will be called upon to determine if a gag suit that merits quick dismissal constitutes *in addition* a SLAPP requiring the application of a punishment of the parties that instigated the proceedings.

The conceptual clarification proposed above now takes on its full meaning. A gag suit is one that unduly hinders the social or political participation of the defendant. It has adverse social and political effects that need to be curbed quickly through a prompt dismissal of the proceedings initiated, the financial protection of parties being targeted and the compensation, where applicable, of those parties, for example, through reimbursement of costs incurred.

The court would thus be called upon to qualify a legal action as a gag suit on the basis of objective criteria:

1. Nature of the activities carried out by the defendant for which the lawsuit was instigated;
2. Determination of the social and political context within which the lawsuit is instigated; and
3. Current or anticipated effects of this suit on the conduct of the defendant's activities.

On the other hand, a strategic lawsuit against public participation is one of which the *main objective* is the intimidation or legal repression of political adversaries. It is thus up to the court that has previously qualified a proceeding as a gag suit to determine if the elements of the case before it permit it to declare the suit abusive. The process used by the court would be deductive and would have to recognize the existence:

1. Of a probability of improper intentions on the part of the plaintiff through an analysis of the case before it and the legal actions instituted against the defendant, and, in particular;
2. Of a disproportion, either in the relationship between the fault the plaintiff alleges to be a victim of and the damages claimed, or in the scale of the proceedings instigated and the resources deployed by the plaintiff in the legal arena.

Anti-gag measures should protect and compensate citizens dragged into the legal system following public participation. Their objectives are to avoid the weakening of that participation and to ensure to some degree the vitality of the democratic process. The prevention of SLAPPs should function in the same way, but involves two additional fundamental precepts: dissuasion and punishment. This means, on the one hand, acting proactively and discouraging individuals and institutions that might be tempted to attempt strategies of legal intimidation from using this method. This is accomplished essentially through the addition of a legal risk to the process, that is, the institution of proceedings permitting the rapid identification of SLAPPs and the creation of a mechanism for financial penalization. This penalization, which comes after the fact, should not only lead to compensation for the victim, but also discourage the party that instigated abusive proceedings from using this method of intimidation again. Such measures would send to the community a clear message that this kind of legal action will not be tolerated.

Summary

This book is concerned with the two-fold phenomenon of legal intimidation and the judicialization of public debates. It problematizes the use of the courts in public debates as a tool of censorship that can weaken and distort citizen participation in political life. The concept of the strategic lawsuit against public participation (SLAPP) remains the conceptual tool par excellence used by experts and legislators to refer to attempts at the legal muzzling of expression related to issues of public interest. How the term is used, however, is inconsistent. Some see in SLAPPs action that has no foundation. Others consider that the necessary protection of freedom of expression calls for the elimination of the criterion of intentionality. I am opposed to these two proposals: attempts at legal intimidation can very well capitalize on errors in law by referring matters to the courts for political purposes. Moreover, the elimination of the concept of intention hinders a discussion both on the translation of relationships of economic domination into legal domination and on the repression of social and political activism by the actors, or the classes of actors, who possess the legal capital required.

It is therefore preferable to differentiate between SLAPPs and gag suits. A SLAPP is an intentional action of intimidation and legal repression; a gag suit is associated with the judicialization and privatization of disputes emerging during public debates. The social and political effects of these lawsuits are analogous, although their legal and political issues differ. SLAPPs can be seen as a greater threat than gag suits since they constitute an attempt to deliberately and abusively co-opt legal proceedings for political purposes.

Laws written to deal with SLAPPs frequently run into problems. They commonly require that the party targeted by a suit that it identifies as a SLAPP demonstrate the abusive or malicious nature of the legal action. This task is difficult, and borderline cases therefore tend to remain before the courts. The most promising legislative models give priority to the prompt dismissal of gag suits (legal proceedings the existence of which is evaluated on the basis of objective criteria), and then the penalization of strategic lawsuits against public participation (namely, gag suits for which the courts have ruled on their abusive or malicious nature through a deductive process).

The following chapters will provide more details on SLAPPs, the primary subject of the analysis proposed in this book, and the different legislative models considered or adopted in order to curtail this phenomenon of legal intimidation.

Notes

1. This definition is based largely on the work of three Quebec academics. See MacDonald et al. 2007: 7.
2. I therefore repeat the argument of Vick and Campbell (2001) and maintain that the legal foundation of the case is not an integral part of an appropriate definition of the

concept of SLAPP. In Chapter 3, I will analyze a Canadian case identified in the literature as a SLAPP in which allegations of defamation were upheld against the defendant.
3. On the issue of the inclusion of the criterion of intentionality in the concept of strategic lawsuit against public participation, see, for example, Braun (2003: 731–83).
4. At the beginning of the 1990s, the Shell oil company, for example, was forced to pay more than 7.5 million dollars in compensation, lawyers' fees and punitive damages to two individuals whom it had sued maliciously. See *Leonardini v. Shell Oil Co.* 1989.
5. See *2332-4197 Québec inc., 2958597 Canada inc., Gilles Proulx et Denzil Thom c. Serge Galipeau et Christine Landry*, 2006.
6. The operating licence for the site was revoked in 2006 by the Minister of the Environment, putting a stop to the landfill operations. See Société Radio-Canada 2006, September 21.
7. *2332-4197 Québec inc. c. Galipeau* 2010 QCCS 3427, para. 44.
8. See decision of the Superior Court on the issue. *2332-4197 Québec inc. c. Galipeau* 2010 QCCS 3427. Superior Court of Québec, April 18, 2011. See also Thériault 2011, February 21.
9. When this was being written, Serge Galipeau and Christine Landry still had not received any financial compensation.
10. See, for example, *Eastern Railroad Presidents Conference v. Noerr Motor Freight, Inc.* 365 U.S. 127, 1961; *United Mine Workers v. Pennington* 381 U.S. 657 (1965); and *Columbia v. Omni Outdoor Advertising, Inc.* 499 U.S. 365, 1991.
11. The right to petition is, however, protected in Quebec by section 21 of the *Charter of Human Rights and Freedoms*. However, in Quebec law, it plays a more limited role than in the United States.
12. This is the case, for instance, in Quebec. The procedural impropriety "may consist in a claim or pleading that is clearly unfounded, frivolous or dilatory or in conduct that is vexatious or quarrelsome. It may also consist in bad faith, in a use of procedure that is excessive or unreasonable or causes prejudice to another person, or in an attempt to defeat the ends of justice, in particular if it restricts freedom of expression in public debate" (Civil Code of Québec, S.Q., section 54.1).
13. The main question consisted then of determining what would be eventually considered as a "probability of intention" and "a realistic possibility" of improper intention sufficient for the court. We will look at these legislative models in more detail in Chapter 3.
14. See, for example, *Minnesota Statutes 2009*, chapter 554: Free speech: Participation in the government. Online: <https://www.revisor.mn.gov/data/revisor/statute/2009/554/2009-554.pdf>.
15. This is in fact a frequent outcome: public debates regularly lead to a focus on the private interests of the actors involved. For example, a forestry company will see a blockade of logging roads as interference with its business, a promoter will identify the organization of public resistance to his projects as a conspiracy, or a politician will consider questioning of his motifs, interests and allegiances as defamation. Disputes are framed from a perspective of affirmation of private rights against actors thinking in terms of participation and political debate.
16. The right to reputation is, for example, invoked by many political stakeholders in order to "set the record straight" and impose their specific perspectives on complex issues in which they are actors — tasks that frequently deserve to be entrusted to a public

functioning as judge and actor in processes that define the public interest.
17. There is nothing very new in what is being suggested here; the first possible solution was proposed more than a decade ago, unfortunately without much success, in Australia.

Chapter 2

The Mechanisms and Processes of SLAPPs

Those who want to treat a disease have to first know its characteristics and causes. This chapter looks in detail at strategic lawsuits against public participation and presents their mechanisms and processes.

The concept of SLAPP refers to the political instrumentalization of the legal system in order to limit, restrict or prevent free speech or activities undertaken by citizens on an issue of public interest. This strategy is based essentially on the forced movement of activists, opponents, intellectuals, protestors or ordinary citizens from a public arena of debate to a legal arena for the resolution of disputes (see Canan 1989).

The process is essentially as follows: one party declares itself the victim of an infringement of its rights in relationship to a public controversy, and institutes a civil suit demanding from an opposing party a sizeable monetary compensation. This compensation is supposed to make up for damage the plaintiff claims to have suffered through the questioning, denunciation or public protest of its current or planned activities. The assertion of damages suffered is a pretext for, and has the consequence of, removing adversaries from a political — and therefore public — arena and confining them to a private legal arena. By doing this, the instigator of the lawsuit uses the characteristics of the judicial process (in particular its slowness, the excessive cost of its proceedings, the formal, technical and procedural weight of its standards and its private and frequently confidential nature) in order to impose its will in a political arena, to punish opponents and to intimidate those who might be tempted to oppose it.

It appears that the roots of this evil lie in the United States (see Pring and Canan 1996; Macdonald et al. 2007; Wells 1998), although it is likely that SLAPP-like phenomena also existed at the same time in other countries. The researchers who developed the concept of SLAPP maintain among other things that such lawsuits existed shortly after American independence, although this practice was marginal until the second half of the twentieth century (see Pring and Canan 1996). The re-emergence of the phenomenon since the 1960s can be attributed to a specific legal culture that is quick to judicialize social and political conflicts as well as a re-alignment of the power relations among social, economic and political agents. This shift in power relationships resulted in particular from a wave of social mobilization around issues of civil and political rights, from the growth of the non-profit sector as a political force, and from the use by citizens of effective public relations and media strategies against adversaries possessing greater financial and political capital (see, for example, Abell 1993; Goetz 1992). SLAPPs thus appeared in the North American context as an option available to actors possessing substantial legal and financial capital (and more specifically corporations, promoters and merchants) that permitted them to respond judicially to the extensive political and media influence of civil society groups.

It is difficult to precisely evaluate the scope of the phenomenon observed in the United States in recent decades. American experts, however, estimated in the mid-1990s that thousands of SLAPPs had been instigated during the two decades prior, that tens of thousands of Americans had been victims of them and that many more had been gagged by the threat of legal reprisals.[1] The problem was identified as serious and epidemic, requiring a rapid response that would provide an antidote to what had become a dysfunctional political system marked by the pathological expansion of the legal system into social and political domains:

> A new breed of lawsuits is stalking America. Like some new strain of virus, these court cases carry dire consequences for individuals, communities and the body politic. Americans by the thousands are being sued, simply for exercising one of our most cherished rights: the right to communicate our views to our government officials, to "speak out" on public issues. Today, you and your friends, neighbors, co-workers, community leaders, and clients can be sued for millions of dollars just for telling the government what you think, want, or believe in. Both individuals and groups are now being routinely sued in multimillion-dollar damage actions for such "all-American" political activities as circulating a petition, writing a letter to the editor, testifying at a public hearing, reporting violations of law, lobbying for legislation, peaceful demonstrating, or otherwise attempting to influence government action. And even though the vast majority of such suits fail in court, they often succeed in the "real world" by silencing citizens and groups, with potentially grave consequences for the future of representative democracy. (Pring and Canan 1996: 1–2)

Recognition by the legal and legislative elites in North American of the existence of this strategy of legal oppression is relatively recent. Nonetheless, at this time and following research and ongoing political lobbying by academics, activists, jurists and legislators, twenty-nine American states, districts and territories have adopted anti-SLAPP legislative mechanisms.[2] A federal bill that was supposed to standardize protections against these lawsuits was presented to the American Congress in 2009.[3] While the United States remains the epicentre of the problem, it is also the country where the most energetic measures have been taken to counteract the abusive instrumentalization of the courts. The protections offered by various American jurisdictions are, however, far from equivalent and much remains to be done to curtail the phenomenon.

In order to better understand the legal mechanisms put in place by the legislation adopted in the United States and being considered elsewhere in the world (which will be presented in the next chapter), we will first have to better describe the phenomenon that such mechanisms are intended to counteract.

An Established Formula

SLAPPs follow an established formula and usually take place in three stages. Citizens, mobilizing around an issue of public interest, publicly express their concerns, oppositions or opinions to audiences that they consider appropriate (voters, members of their communities, media, legislators, community leaders, etc.[4]). By doing so, they come into conflict with the interests of a private or public party, often embodied by a promoter, a corporation or a government agency. This adversary is not able to control or dominate the public debate on its current actions or future projects.

Struggling to impose its position in the political arena, this adversary decides to make a direct legal counterattack against its detractors. It invokes some kind of damages resulting from actions, gestures or communications by its opponents and requiring compensation before a court. The SLAPPer goes on the offensive.

This process is eminently political and results in three shifts:

1. First of all, it transforms the political participation of the targeted parties (frequently, although not always, protected by constitutional provisions) into legal damages. This occurs through the frequent reference to some kind of harm: defamation, interference in contractual business, violation of private property, nuisance or conspiracy. This is a transformation of the *matter* under dispute. The conflict is no longer, for example, about the relevance of the construction of a large-scale residential development in a quiet neighbourhood, but about the legitimacy of the interventions and actions of the opponents to the project.
2. Second, this process shifts the dispute in question from a public political arena to a private legal arena. It means changing the *forum* of the dispute. This shift results in the parties being confined to a costly, slow, opaque arena. This second transformation imposes on the parties targeted by lawsuits a set of norms, procedures and legal proceedings that are supposed to intimidate and demotivate them, and exhaust them psychologically and financially. The legal process then has the effect of dispossessing the SLAPP victims of their cases and of any real power to act, since they have to place their fate in the hands of a lawyer with whom they associate as a client. The confinement of political adversaries to a legal system is thus used to permit the SLAPPer to weaken its adversaries or punish them for having gotten in its way.
3. Finally, this process transforms a public political issue into a private legal issue, through a process of *judicial privatization of public debates*. The instigator of the SLAPP converts an essentially political (and therefore of public interest)

dispute into a private conflict. The parties targeted by the suit risk not only seeing the projects or ideas they oppose come to fruition, but also losing their houses, savings and reputations, since a legal conviction carries the brand of public censure and official sanction. It means transforming the *issues* of the dispute (see Pring and Canan 1996; Ericson-Siegel 1992; Wells 1998; Canan 1989).

The third and final step of a SLAPP is the actual judicial proceedings. These usually drag on for months, even years, draining the energies and resources of the citizens being sued. The slowness of the proceedings serves the interests of the party that has instigated the lawsuit, exhausting its adversary. As the case may be, the lawsuit will eventually be dropped by the plaintiff, the parties will reach an out-of court settlement or a judgment on the merits will be made by a court. We will examine this in detail below.

Through this process, SLAPPs invert the offensive and defensive relationships that have traditionally characterized political disputes. The plaintiff, previously forced to defend actions, projects or ideas in the public arena, thus goes from a *politically defensive position* to a *judicially offensive position*. Consequently, the citizens, groups or organizations opposing it go from a politically offensive position of questioning and denunciation to a judicially defensive position of justification, defence and/or retreat. This inversion of the offensive and defensive relationships permits the instigator of the lawsuit to impose itself politically in a public arena over which it previously had had little control (see McBride 1993; Baruch 1996). A SLAPP is therefore an instrument to invert existing power relationships:

> A SLAPP gives its filer an opportunity to regain the upper hand in a dispute which it is losing in the political arena. It can also recast the terms of the dispute. Whereas in the political realm the filer is typically on the defensive, in the legal realm the filer can go on the offensive, putting the targets' actions under scrutiny. (Tollefson 1994: 207)

The first answer to the question "how does a strategic lawsuit against public participation work?" will therefore be: through the deliberate instrumentalization of judicial proceedings as a weapon of intimidation, censorship and/or political reprisal in the context of social and political conflicts. The functioning and internal logic of SLAPPs thus become clear: they are based on the inversion of the offensive and defensive relationships between adversaries through the forced shift of citizens from a political, public arena to a legal, private arena. The legal process gives the party that instigated the SLAPP a decisive strategic advantage in the conduct of its activities. This advantage is based on:

1) The inequality of the resources that the opposing parties can deploy;
2) The diversion, and eventually the exhaustion, of the adversary's resources;

3) The intimidation of the members of communities the defendant parties belong to[5];
4) The moral and psychological exhaustion of the targeted parties, caused by the dissolution of boundaries between their public and private lives. (Barker 1993; Pring and Canan 1996)

The fourth and final aspect (the moral and psychological exhaustion of the victims of SLAPPs) is based on the incorporation into the legal dispute of the capital and private property of the SLAPPed individuals. The family, community and professional lives of the targeted parties become entangled in a now private conflict. This leads, ultimately, to the development of tensions in family, professional and community relations.[6] The violence suffered by the victims of SLAPPs greatly exceeds the simple financial domain and includes significant social, psychological and emotional damage:

> Potential extralegal outcomes, such as the costs of lawsuit defence, other monetary losses, the personal costs of psychological trauma and of undermined belief in political participation, the ripple effect on other citizens' political involvement, and the diversion of resources from the original issue in dispute. (Canan and Pring 1988: 390)

Although frequently associated with the environmental protection sector in Quebec and Canada, SLAPPs are aimed at all participants expressing themselves in the public arena on potentially controversial issues. Citizens, researchers, professors, journalists, activists and politicians are all potential targets of such legal actions.[7] In addition, the phenomenon of strategic lawsuits against public participation does not involve, contrary to the image frequently evoked, only large commercial or industrial corporations suing citizens or isolated groups. This strategy is also used by government agencies who want to stifle controversy, by smaller entrepreneurs who are facing effective social opposition and by actors in positions of public responsibility whose actions are controversial (police officers, elected officials at various levels, actors working in the health sector, educators, etc.). As a specific legal practice, SLAPPs are thus used by a large number of social, economic and political actors.

Problematic cases have appeared in Quebec in which the legal actions initiated by politicians have been considered attempts at legal intimidation.[8] The ex-Minister of Justice of Quebec, Marc Bellemare, for example, claimed that a suit filed against him in April 2010 by the Premier of Quebec was the equivalent of a "gag suit" that was supposed to "gag" him and "intimidate" him.[9] The mayor of Quebec City also provoked anger and indignation from the Fédération professionnelle des journalistes du Québec (FPJQ) in February 2011 by announcing that his party would sue when he felt he was the target of false allegations or damage to his reputation. For the FPJQ, this was an "attempt at intimidation as unjustifiable as it is unacceptable" that had "the appearance of a pre-emptive gag suit."[10] These examples illustrate the existence of a wider problem of the legal contamination of public debate generated by the judicialization of private conflicts arising out of public controversies.

Social and Political Consequences of SLAPPs

The social and political consequences of strategic lawsuits against public participation are serious and often lead to the depoliticization of their victims' entire communities (see, for example, Stein 1989). The impact of SLAPPs on public participation can thus be seen as two-fold. They attack, first of all, the individuals targeted by the abusive lawsuits. The victims of such lawsuits are "frequently devastated and depoliticized and discourage others from speaking out" (Pring and Canan 1996: xi). This is explained by the prolonged stress and the considerable — in particular financial — risk imposed on them.[11] Second, although strategic lawsuits against public participation are frequently aimed at a limited number of individuals or organizations, they have the effect of constraining, perverting and seriously limiting public debate by silencing the communities where their victims live.[12] The process of legal intimidation thus pushes entire communities into self-censorship.[13] This consequence is eminently political and contributes to social disengagement in the short and long term:

> SLAPP suits function by forcing the target into the judicial arena where the SLAPP filer foists upon the target the expenses of a defence. The longer the litigation can be stretched out, the more litigation that can be churned, the greater the expense that is inflicted and the closer the SLAPP filer moves to success.... The ripple effect of such suits in our society is enormous. Persons who have been outspoken on issues of public importance targeted in such suits or who have witnessed such suits will often choose in the future to stay silent. (*Gordon v. Marrone 1992*. Quoted by Lott 2004)[14]

In summary, it can be observed that:

- SLAPPs muzzle public opinion and limit citizen participation in the discussion of public affairs in the short and long term;
- They function as significant *de facto* restrictions, notwithstanding the legal protections in effect, on the capacity of the citizens and groups targeted by such lawsuits to express themselves on issues of public interest;
- They result in personal, emotional and financial damage for the families and friends of the people targeted by such lawsuits;
- There is a danger that they will lead to gradual depoliticization of citizens who have suffered from or observed a SLAPP, or at least to excessive prudence in their social and political actions.

"In the end, we are being made an example in order to frighten everyone." —André Bélisle, president of the Association québécoise de lutte contre la pollution atmosphérique (AQLPA)

The case began in May 2005. The Association québécoise de lutte contre la pollution atmosphérique (AQLPA) and the Comité de restauration de la rivière Etchemin (CRRE) were notified about the presence of suspicious discharges into the Etchemin River. These organizations had been working for years to restore the river and reintroduce salmon, a local species that had disappeared from the waterway due to prolonged pollution. There was a lot of concern in these groups: the discharges could imperil the entire program, which until then had had excellent results (Société Radio-Canada 2006, October 3).

The AQLPA and the CRRE therefore started investigating and discovered that a dry materials dump had been created close to many of the salmon pools that could be used as spawning sites. The dump was run by a scrap metal company. After making checks, the environmentalists found out that the scrap metal company did not have the permits required to operate on the site and that it had not conducted the environmental studies required by regulatory agencies. The groups then turned to the municipal authorities and tried to convince them to force the scrap metal company to respect the regulations in effect. The municipality was slow to act. They met with the same inaction when they approached the Quebec Ministry of Sustainable Development, Environment and Parks. The environmentalists decided to take matters into their own hands (see AQLPA and CRRE 2008).

The AQLPA and the CRRE applied for interlocutory and permanent injunctions with the Superior Court of Québec, and asked that certain administrative measures be cancelled. The interim interlocutory injunction was granted to them in July 2005 (*Association québécoise de lutte contre la pollution atmosphérique (AQLPA) v. Cie américaine de fer et métaux inc. (AIM)*, 2005 CanLII 32531 (QC CS)). When it expired, a safeguard order was issued, then renewed several times by the court.[15] Offence notices were also issued by the Ministry of Sustainable Development, Environment and Parks during the summer of 2005. In total, the work of the company would be suspended for many weeks to give it time to comply with the laws and standards in effect.

The scrap metal company, however, responded to the environmental organizations in November 2005 with a suit of more than five million dollars against the AQLPA, the CRRE and citizens involved in contesting the legality of the company's actions. It was in particular alleged that the parties had conspired with a competitor and damaged the reputation of the company, and claimed that it had suffered an unjustified loss in profits as a result of the activities of the environmental groups (see Bourgault-Côté 2006).

> The case then took a political turn. The following year, the AQLPA and the CRRE launched a huge campaign on the issue of strategic lawsuits against public participation and demanded the adoption of a law to curb the phenomenon. This campaign, as well as its political and legislative results, will be detailed in Chapter 4.
>
> A confidential out-of-court settlement would be concluded between the parties in December 2007. Subsequently, the AQLPA would publicly criticize out-of-court settlements resulting from SLAPP-like lawsuits, since they frequently indicate the psychological and financial exhaustion of the defendant rather than a consensual agreement negotiated between equal parties.

Studies in the United States have demonstrated these effects (see Canan 1989; Pring and Canan 1996). The legal, political and social concerns associated with SLAPPs greatly exceed the context of the individual rights and freedoms of their victims: they represent a growing threat for citizen participation in public debate and the maintenance of the legitimacy of the legal system in liberal democracies.

The Legal and Political Logic of SLAPPs

Strategic lawsuits against public participation are based essentially on two complementary and closely associated logics. The first one is legal and instrumentalizes the tension between *judicial proceedings* and *substantive law*. Judicial proceedings consist in the set of norms, rules and customs that prevail in the course of a legal dispute. Substantive law is made up of all the rules defining the rights and duties of the parties. Judicial proceedings are supposed to permit the hearing of a legal dispute considered equitable and that will theoretically lead to a judgment based on a substantive analysis of the law — in other words, a court ruling based on an interpretation of the rights and duties of the opposing parties.

SLAPPs break this link between judicial proceedings and substantive law by using the process in a way that undermines, violates or limits the exercise of rights protected and recognized by the legal system. This is accomplished essentially by using the judicial proceedings not as a mechanism to ensure the smooth settlement of the legal dispute, but rather as a weapon of political oppression aimed at demobilizing, disorienting, impoverishing and weakening specific adversaries. SLAPPs thus disconnect and distort the relationship between judicial proceedings and substantive law and lead to the crushing of social and political dissidence through the exploitation of flaws in the contemporary legal apparatus.

SLAPPs also function through the creation of legal risks in the domain of public debate. The victims of SLAPPs are forced to operate in a world that is not only foreign but inhospitable to them. They are obliged (and this is not insignificant) to function in a specific setting where they do not usually master the language. This legal language, highly specialized and beyond the understanding of ordinary people, is also a factor that creates anxiety among SLAPP victims; they have to learn to decipher legal discourse related to their cases and reinterpret their actions and words from the perspective of this language and the standards it conveys. All these eventualities, ambiguities and uncertainties fuel the nervousness of citizens being sued for expressing themselves on public controversies:

> This chilling effect comes from both the confusion about being thrown into a foreign system and from the financial threats to defendants. When a case is begun there are endless phone calls and meetings as defendants scramble to try to understand the legal claims made against them. The sums of money involved are truly scary for many people who risk losing houses and life savings, sometimes over fairly trivial allegations or complaints about perhaps one sentence out of countless statements made in the course of a campaign. (Ogle 2005: 10)

Participation in public debates usually assumes acceptance of a certain level of political risk. The *additional* risks associated with SLAPPs can have significant effects on the individual lives and financial stability of citizens taking part in public debates, dissuading public participation. SLAPPs thus bring about a process of *legal privatization of the costs* associated with the political participation of citizen. They involve dimensions traditionally associated with the private lives of citizens (and more specifically the personal capital they possess) as part of a political conflict that has been transformed into a legal dispute.[16] The tension created between, on the one hand, the public domain of the debate and the political controversy, and on the other hand, the private domain of the legal dispute, is at the heart of the process of gagging social and political opposition.

SLAPPs as a Problematic of Legal Intimidation

The strategic lawsuit against public participation is symptomatic of a broader problem of legal intimidation, a process through which one or more actors attempt to impose, limit or prohibit behaviours and actions through threats or the conduct of legal proceedings. The phenomenon is observed in various fields of activity and is not limited to political controversies.[17] SLAPPs represent a particularly well-developed form of legal intimidation intended to gag political opponents.

It is inevitable, in the conduct of their social and political activities, that citizens and non-governmental organizations clash with private and public interests. In doing so, they oppose actors that possess financial and legal resources that are far more substantial than theirs. The latter carry out a risk analysis and respond, when they find it advantageous, with attempts at legal intimidation. This can be seen in the tactical use of formal notices, in unfounded applications for injunctions, in the practice of instigating, then quickly dropping, legal proceedings against groups and individuals who do not possess the financial resources required to deal with a legal dispute. Therefore efforts at legal intimidation do not need to necessarily lead to the development of strategic lawsuits against public participation to be effective. The simple threat of such lawsuits is frequently enough to discourage social mobilization.

This strategy is based on an evaluation of the disparities of resources that can be devoted by the different parties to a legal dispute and takes advantage of a broader problem of unequal access to justice. Lack of access to justice remains one of the biggest problems affecting contemporary liberal democracies.[18] The prohibitive costs associated with legal disputes present a major obstacle to accessibility and equity in legal matters. The instrumentalization of the inequalities of wealth between legal and private persons therefore creates judicial inequality: the legal process expresses, rather than suspends, unequal social relationships marked by the precedence of a limited number of actors who possess the capital required for predominance in this arena (see Chapter 5; also see Canan 1989).

Between Masquerade and Strategy

SLAPPs are understood essentially, in Quebec, Canada and the United States, as attempts to *divert the legal system* to make it a weapon of political oppression. This diversion, as we have seen, is based on the instrumentalization of a certain number of characteristics of the legal arena — its technical, formal, opaque and onerous nature — in order to crush social and political dissidence. It involves the use of proceedings and the legal system for purposes other than those officially attributed to them: to serve justice. This diversion could not work effectively if plaintiffs were not able to give their judicial proceedings a semblance of legitimacy and legal foundation to permit them to circumvent the vigilance of the courts, which have a certain number of tools for the dismissal of abusive lawsuits and penalization of their instigators.

Thus strategic lawsuits against public participation are frequently masquerades, undertakings aimed at camouflaging political intentions behind a legal mask to give at least the minimal semblance of legal foundation and/or legitimacy (see, for example, Huling 1994). The most effective SLAPPs are without a doubt those that conceal most carefully and convincingly the political aims of their instigators. This happens in particular when the party that has instigated the SLAPP instrumentalizes an offence committed by the defendant in the course of his or her public actions to justify and support its legal action. As Abrams writes:

> The problem of retaliatory lawsuits is an extremely complex one, particularly because of the various forms these suits take. They range from obviously frivolous allegations which involve blatant attacks on constitutionally protected free speech and the right to petition the government for redress of grievances, to much more subtle attacks involving allegations of malicious prosecution or interference with business relationships. (Abrams 1989: 33–34)

It thus becomes difficult for a court to determine at the preliminary stages of the hearing if the case before it is actually lacking any legal foundation or if it is hiding illegitimate intentions that are *other* than success on substance (in this case, the diversion of the legal system for political purposes) (see Sills 1993). Similarly, since the lawsuit is presented as an essentially private matter between two private parties, it is difficult for the courts to rule on the political and abusive nature of the legal action undertaken when the defendant does not reformulate the proceedings undertaken against it as an attack on his or her political rights. SLAPPs have to be unmasked and presented as attempts at political oppression in order to be promptly rejected by the courts. We will see in the following chapter that the legal traditions of common law and civil law in effect in Canada do not favour the quick dismissal of such lawsuits.

Possible Conclusions

In general, a strategic lawsuit against public participation can be decided in four ways: 1) the quick dismissal of the lawsuit by the court; 2) the eventual abandonment of the lawsuit by the plaintiff; 3) the prolongation of the case until its final conclusion in a trial; or 4) the negotiation of an out-of-court settlement between the parties by which they agree to halt the legal proceedings.

The inability of the different legal systems to ensure the quick dismissal of strategic lawsuits against public participation is the reason for the various legislative initiatives undertaken in North America over the last few decades in order to counteract the phenomenon (see Chapter 3). In the absence of effective legislation to ensure the quick dismissal of SLAPPs, there is a danger that they will continue to be permitted if they maintain the appearance of legitimacy or legal foundation.

It is important, however, to mention that most SLAPPs never reach the point of a final judgment, since the parties tend to reach out-of-court settlements or plaintiffs eventually drop the lawsuits. The abandonment of legal proceedings undertaken by the plaintiffs after a certain amount of time can be part of a legal or political strategy. This can occur at a time preceding a key stage in the legal process (in order to avoid additional costs or an unfavourable decision); it can also result in the attainment of the political objectives outside the legal dispute — either victory on the initial issue under dispute, diversion or exhaustion, or effective stifling of social and political opposition. Strategic withdrawal from the legal dispute can in this way serve the interests of the party that instigated the SLAPP just as much as the launching of the judicial proceedings in themselves. This abandonment therefore does not mean a setback for the party that instituted the proceedings: it may have been planned or anticipated in conjunction with extralegal objectives:

> By the time the filers lose (typically years later if there is no effective anti-SLAPP statute in force, or if it is not invoked) or settle (ordinarily

after the opposition has run out of money, or energy, or activists), their objectives of intimidation and of shifting the forum and issues to ones of their choosing have usually been accomplished. (Braun 1999: 971)

Victory on substance can still be given to the plaintiff — the instigator of the SLAPP — if the defendants actually committed a legal fault and if they failed to present both their initial activities and the issues of the lawsuit not from a strictly legal perspective, based on a private dispute, but rather political, related to their rights and fundamental freedoms. This omission can result in the courts not considering the constitutional or quasi constitutional protections given to political activities (demonstrations, public speech, petitions, publication of opinions and political analyses, etc.), something crucial in a democracy, written into the constitution, protected by the various charters in effect in the country, and recognized by jurisprudence. Things also get complicated in Canada, where the legal system favours the balance of contradictory rights. This quest for balance and conciliation between competing rights makes it more difficult to dismiss proceedings that interfere with political rights; such cases are evaluated by the courts taking into account other rights (and in particular the right to reputation) before restricting and limiting them. In addition, as we will soon see below, the limited scope of the Canadian *Charter of Rights and Freedoms* significantly limits the extent of constitutional protection against SLAPPs.

It can happen that the plaintiff, after months and even years of slow, costly and tedious legal preparation, proposes to the defendant an out-of-court agreement to officialize a settlement between the parties. The terms of this settlement are usually negotiated according to the level of moral, psychological and financial exhaustion of the defendant. The economic inequalities between the parties — their abilities to cover, over a long period of time, the costs related to the legal dispute — influence the power relationships on the basis of which the terms of an out-of-court agreement can be negotiated. These out-of-court settlements, which are supposed to officially conclude a free and consensual agreement between the parties, can hide, under the appearance of a healthy resolution of a conflict between private parties, the outcome of legal intimidation taken to its conclusion.[19]

The Question of Damages and Compensation

In the absence of specific legislation to counteract the phenomenon, SLAPP victims in Canada usually recover a small proportion of the total legal costs incurred and are rarely awarded punitive and exemplary damages. Lawyer's fees, which currently constitute the highest costs of any legal defence, are rarely recovered by the defendants, even when they win their cases in court. Only a judgment that rules on *both* the legitimacy of the defendants' activities and actions and the obviously abusive nature of the legal action taken against them would make possible appropriate financial compensation.

> "Me, I had a warrior spirit. I said to myself: it won't happen this way. They won't be able to shut me up. My lawyer told me: 'Keep quiet, Sébastien. It could work against you. Mandate someone else to speak, but you have to stop talking.' That's what you call a gag. It worked." — Sébastien Lussier, spokesperson for a committee of citizens opposing the activities of a company recycling solid waste. (Lussier 2008)

Describing an odour can prove to be dangerous for anyone who dares to do so at the expense of those wealthier than him. Sébastien Lussier would learn this lesson well in spite of himself in May 2006.

Exasperated by nauseating smells, he joined a committee of citizens affected by the emissions produced by Ferti-Val Inc., a company specializing in the recycling of solid waste operating close to residential neighbourhoods in the Brompton Borough of the City of Sherbrooke, in the Eastern Townships. Sébastien Lussier would become the spokesperson for the committee. Citizen discontent about the smells caused by the business was then palpable. In April 2006, more than a thousand citizens signed a petition demanding the closure of the business (see *La Tribune* 2006). The City of Sherbrooke, realizing there was a problem, also issued the company seventeen offence notices in one year (see Société Radio-Canada 2006, December 20).

Expressing himself from time to time in the local media about the activities of Ferti-Val, Sébastien Lussier focused on denouncing the nauseating nature of the smells of "putrefaction" coming from the site. The company was not happy about this. It responded vigorously, calling the allegations of the spokesperson "distortions," "libellous" and "completely erroneous" (Bombardier 2006, December 15a; Bombardier 2006, May 17; Bombardier 2006, December 15b).

The company therefore demanded compensation. Sébastien Lussier was sued for $700,000. The impact of the lawsuit on the debate around the smells coming from Ferti-Val was immediate. On the advice of his lawyer, the spokesperson of the citizens had to turn down requests for interviews from the media (both regarding the lawsuit and the initial dispute) until the conclusion of the legal proceedings against him. The citizens in the area then began to be extremely cautious in their comments about the smells produced by the company (see Société Radio-Canada 2006, October 3).

Ferti-Val dropped the lawsuit against Sébastien Lussier in November 2006, pled guilty the next month in municipal court to charges against it by the City of Sherbrooke and took measures to comply with the regulations in effect.[20]

This being said, defendants who feel they are the victims of an attempt at legal muzzling can, while defending themselves against the original suit, take legal action against the plaintiff, alleging that the original lawsuits instigated against them were malicious or excessive. This strategy, imported from the United States and commonly called "SLAPP-back" (see Costantini and Nash 1991), has four objectives:

1. Recover the costs associated with the legal defence;
2. Intimidate the plaintiff and put it on the defensive;
3. Reaffirm publicly the legitimacy of the public actions for which the defendant was sued and send a public signal of non-intimidation;
4. Dissuade those who had instigated SLAPPs, or those who might be tempted to, from using this form of legal intimidation in the future.

This process has obvious strategic value. It realigns the offensive and defensive relationships between the adversaries, opens up a new legal front where the party that instigated the SLAPP is forced to operate and permits social remobilization around a suit that is a legal response to a social and political injustice. This being said, this strategy remains the prerogative of groups and citizens who possess the psychological, financial, material and time resources required to carry it out (this kind of case requires a high level of personal investment). Citizens and organizations that have more modest resources or that are already exhausted by their defence will not be able to take this route (see Huling 1994; Stetson 1995). Therefore it has limited applications.

Obtaining punitive and exemplary damages is, in fact, a difficult and uncertain and often long and very onerous process for defendants in SLAPP cases. It requires demonstrating the abusive or malicious nature of the legal proceedings introduced by the party that instigated the SLAPP; the court has to deduce the intentions of the party that instituted the legal proceedings on the basis of the substance of the legal case or how the proceedings are used (Barker 1993; Huling 1994). The illegitimate intentions of the plaintiff can thus be demonstrated by the lack of any legal foundation for the case brought to court, or else by the fact that the party that instigated the proceedings maliciously increased the number of legal actions in order to uselessly delay the proceedings, to raise the costs associated with the preparation of the legal case for the defendant, or to weigh down the legal process. The malicious nature of a lawsuit is still, in all cases, difficult to establish.

SLAPP, Law and Democracy: Fundamental Principles

The concepts of access to justice, the right to a fair and equitable trial, freedom of expression, the right to public participation and the right to information are at the heart of the social and political issues raised by SLAPPs.[21] There are generally two aspects to how these concepts are handled. On the one hand, they are frequently invoked politically — they then appear simultaneously as normative ideal, moral principle and political argument — and are used to perform political representations in public space. At the same time, these concepts are also legal provisions defined, framed and delimited by the law, and which can be mobilized in relationship to legal disputes: they are thus evoked legally in order to be imposed in the legal arena. There are sometimes significant discrepancies between the political and legal interpretations of these rights, which can lead to significant social and political controversies.

In other words, *moral and political* appeals to the rights protected by the charters and jurisprudence in effect in the country have to be distinguished, in their substance and how they are affirmed, from *legal references* to them. SLAPPs highlight the sometimes substantial gaps between the moral and legal interpretations of rights. The legal interpretations made by Canadian courts of the right to freedom of expression — an essential principle underlying social mobilization in the country — are thus frequently very distinct from its social and moral interpretations. It is one thing to publicly affirm a right; it is another to obtain a legal decision that confirms this right and defines it accordingly. Few Canadians know, for example, that the rights protected by the Canadian *Charter of Rights and Freedoms* apply only with respect to public authorities and cannot be applied to private conflicts.[22] The context of a SLAPP highlights this gap between social and legal interpretations of the idea of "just and equitable" trial when conflicts are played out in a context of economic imbalance.

In Quebec and Canada, discourse on SLAPPs have been in large part developed around these five concepts: access to justice, the right to a fair and equitable trial, freedom of expression, the right to public participation and the right to information; they are the elements that are essential for an understanding of the problem.

Right to a Fair and Equitable Trial and Access to Justice

The right to a fair and equitable trial is guaranteed by the *Charter of Human Rights and Freedoms* and the *International Covenant on Civil and Political Rights*.[23] The Quebec Charter includes the following provisions in this regard:

> Every person has a right to a full and equal, public and fair hearing by an independent and impartial tribunal, for the determination of his rights and obligations or of the merits of any charge brought against him. (section 23)
>
> Every person has a right to be represented by an advocate or to be assisted by one before any tribunal. (section 34)

These provisions include negative and positive obligations for the Quebec government. It cannot legitimately interfere with a matter that is before the courts to bias the outcome or deprive a person of his or her right to be represented by a lawyer. These negative obligations require the public authorities to respect the independence of the legal system. It is, however, responsible for seeing that public hearings are organized in an equitable and impartial way and ensuring a certain level of accessibility to services of legal representation. This means positive measures requiring investment from the government in the legal system. The creation of a legal aid program and the Fonds d'aide aux recours collectifs [Legal Aid Fund for Class Action Lawsuits] are among the measures adopted by the authorities in order to ensure minimum accessibility to services of legal representation for the population of Quebec.

The concepts of "equality" and "impartiality" raised by these sections of the Charter take on a very different meaning, however, when we consider the huge imbalance of the forces that our legal system permits (and therefore endorses) in relationship to cases presented before it. It is difficult to conceive of an equitable and impartial legal dispute when there are such huge imbalances between the parties.

There are two aspects to the problem. On the one hand, problems of access to justice are recurrent in Quebec, in spite of the measures implemented in recent decades to mitigate its severity.[24] The adoption of the *Legal Aid Act* in the early 1970s and the subsequent establishment of thresholds giving disadvantaged people access to the services of a lawyer was supposed to correct what had become an unacceptable situation. The Minister of Justice at the time, Jérôme Choquette, declared:

> After all, in 1972, any Quebecer who is in a deplorable economic situation has a right to social assistance and any Quebecer has the right to consult a doctor and be treated in a hospital without facing financial ruin. Don't we have the same fundamental duty to see to it that, in the legal domain, those who have urgent need of defence in the legal system and the complex legal apparatus that we now have recognized the right to consultation and assistance when their financial situation does not permit them to fully enjoy their rights as human beings? (quoted by Jarry 2005)

The problem is no nearer to a solution forty years later, since the thresholds of eligibility for legal aid cover only the poorest segments of Quebec society.[25] The costs associated with the financing of legal representation, which frequently amount to hundreds of dollars an hour, will always remain quite prohibitive for large segments of the population.

Moreover, the individuals and corporations that possess the capital necessary for legal representation are capable of investing substantial sums of money in disputes with adversaries who are incapable of assuming similar expenses. SLAPPs represent the instrumentalization of this failure to balance the power relationships since they capitalize on lack of access to justice in order to turn legal proceedings into a weapon that can be deployed against less affluent adversaries.

The *formal* legal equality of the parties (prohibition of giving superior legal status to one of the parties or attributing to one litigant rights and privileges refused to another) as well as the formally equal nature of court hearings (application of the same rules and proceedings to all parties) need to be distinguished from the *actual* capacities of the litigants to mobilize the resources necessary to conduct the legal dispute (see Chapter 5). The existence of sometimes significant disparities in legal capital between the parties therefore creates an inequality of the forces involved, which is not always properly taken into consideration by a legal institution that shows a persistent myopia in this regard. SLAPPs thus oblige us to call into question the concept of legal equity in a context of the unequal distribution of legal capital between various categories of social actors.

Right to Freedom of Expression

The constitutional protection of freedom of expression is considered to be a cornerstone of Canadian democracy. The Canadian *Charter of Rights and Freedoms* stipulates that each Canadian citizen enjoys "freedom of thought, belief, opinion and expression, including freedom of the press and other media of communication." Section 19 of the *International Covenant on Civil and Political Rights*, of which Canada is a signatory since 1976, defines the right to freedom of expression as follows:

> Everyone shall have the right to freedom of expression; this right shall include freedom to seek, receive and impart information and ideas of all kinds, regardless of frontiers, either orally, in writing or in print, in the form of art, or through any other media of his choice.

The distinction to be made between the moral and legal concepts of freedom of expression is important in the context of any discussion on SLAPPs. The preservation of the right to freedom of expression is, in fact, commonly presented as a fundamental issue associated with the abusive strategic instrumentalization of the Canadian legal system. However, the limitations of the Canadian *Charter of Rights and Freedoms* considerably reduce the *judicial appeal* of the constitutional right to freedom of expression as a normative principle that makes it possible to curtail this practice.[26]

Except in Quebec, where the application is broader, freedom of expression is therefore treated in Canada as a right essentially applicable (even almost exclusively) against public authorities. This is a legal principle stipulating that the government, whether federal or provincial, must refrain from limiting or controlling the communications of its citizens if it cannot do so reasonably, through a law, and satisfactorily justify its action. This is therefore of a limited application in conflicts involving private actors (individuals, corporations, non-profit organizations, etc.). Noting these limitations, the Canadian *common law* provinces distanced themselves from anti-SLAPP legislative models focusing on freedom of expression and tried to define a "right of public participation" using a normative principle in order to legitimize the institution of special legal processes. It is important, of course, to examine the relevance and interest of restricting legal applications of freedom of expression to cases involving public authorities. What is more, it seems necessary to evaluate the way in which the right to freedom of expression is diminished and domesticated by an inflated right to reputation. These points will be discussed in more detail in Chapter 3.

Right to Participate in Public Affairs

The right to participate in public affairs, although it has no explicit constitutional value in Canada (it is understood as a constitutive dimension of the right to freedom of expression), is part of the Canadian legal system and is used as a normative principle governing social and political life in the country. It is mobilized both legally and politically in the debates around SLAPPs in Canada.

Article 25 of the *International Covenant on Civil and Political Rights* defines a right to participate in public affairs by stipulating that:

> Every citizen shall have the right and the opportunity, without any of the distinctions mentioned in article 2 and without unreasonable restrictions:
>
> a) To take part in the conduct of public affairs, directly or through freely chosen representatives;
> b) To vote and to be elected at genuine periodic elections which shall be by universal and equal suffrage and shall be held by secret ballot, guaranteeing the free expression of the will of the electors;
> c) To have access, on general terms of equality, to public service in his country.

The United Nations Human Rights Committee[27] clarified these provisions in a general comment on article 25, adopted in 1996. The committee in particular made the following remarks:

> Citizens may participate directly by taking part in popular assemblies which have the power to make decisions about local issues or about the affairs of a particular community and in bodies established to represent citizens in consultation with government. Where a mode of direct participation by citizens is established, no distinction should be made between citizens as regards their participation on the grounds mentioned in article 2, paragraph 1, and no unreasonable restrictions should be imposed. (para. 6) ...
>
> Citizens also take part in the conduct of public affairs by exerting influence through public debate and dialogue with their representatives or through their capacity to organize themselves. This participation is supported by ensuring freedom of expression, assembly and association. (para. 8)
>
> Freedom of expression, assembly and association are essential conditions for the effective exercise of the right to vote and must be fully protected. (para. 12) ...

> In order to ensure the full enjoyment of rights protected by article 25, the free communication of information and ideas about public and political issues between citizens, candidates and elected representatives is essential. This implies a free press and other media able to comment on public issues without censorship or restraint and to inform public opinion. (para. 26)[28]

In addition to equal and non-discriminatory eligibility to public functions and elected positions, the right to participate in public affairs assumes full and complete participation (to the extent prescribed by law) of citizens in public discussions and controversies. It assumes the legitimate integration of an essentially citizen perspective in the public debate and is indissociable from the concept of participatory democracy. The right to participation in public affairs is also closely linked to the right to information and the concept of a free and informed opinion.

Right to Information

The concept of a right to information is polysemic and refers both to a demandable right, a fundamental right, and to a standard right (see Trudel 2001). As a demandable right, the right to information is crystallized, at the federal level, by the *Access to Information Act*.[29] It assumes a certain level of transparency and openness on the part of public institutions to inquiries, requests and questions of citizens of the country with respect to their activities and operating procedures.

The right to information is a fundamental right in Quebec and is stipulated in section 44 of the *Charter of Human Rights and Freedoms*. A right to information is also established, although not explicitly, by the *International Covenant on Civil and Political Rights* since, according to the Covenant, freedom of expression includes the right to "receive and impart information and ideas of all kinds." The Supreme Court of Canada has previously ruled that "it is not only the speaker but the listener who has an interest in freedom of expression" (*Ford v. Quebec (Attorney General)*, 2 S.C.R. 712, 1988). The right to information thus assumes the right to be informed.

Finally, as a standard right, the right to information plays a mediating role between conflicting fundamental rights (between the right to privacy and freedom of the press, for example) and contributes to circumscribing and defining a set of rights that influence each other. The right to information is in line with articles 8 and 26 of the observations made by the Human Rights Committee with respect to the right to take part in the conduct of public affairs; public participation and the right to information are closely connected. The inhibitive effect of strategic lawsuits against public participation (limiting citizen expression and the circulation of information) is therefore opposed to a right to information based on both the rights of *dissemination* and *reception* of information.

Ultimately, the normative principles underlying the discourse on resistance to SLAPPs revolve around three fundamental dimensions of social and political life: express oneself, participate and inform oneself. These principles form the basis for the moral, political and legal arguments used both before the courts and in the public arena to defend positions, legitimize the acts that have led to the filing of lawsuits and problematize them as attacks on the very social and political organization of the community.

In light of the SLAPP's significance, it is important to examine the various legislative initiatives taken in Canada and internationally to counteract the phenomenon. The question, such a sensitive one in Canada, of creating a hierarchy of rights, existing gaps between moral and legal concepts of those rights and limitations imposed on their application, makes it difficult to organize legal solutions in the country. The jurisprudence established by virtue of the Canadian *Charter of Rights and Freedoms* advocates conciliation between rights that could come into conflict and refuses to give precedence to principles of political participation, which still requires a certain prioritization so that they are realized properly. The limitations inherent to the Charter also favour the development of legal solutions that are not based on it. These solutions will be presented and discussed in detail in the next chapter.

Notes

1. The methods for evaluating the number of SLAPPs in the United States by these authors have, however, been subject to significant methodological criticisms (see, for example, Beatty 1993). It is indeed difficult to estimate the number of SLAPPs instigated in a given territory for a specific period. SLAPPs have to, in fact, be recognized *as such* by the defendant or a court; otherwise there is a risk that they will appear to be simple private disputes between two individuals and slip under the radar of the legal system. Accordingly, courts will have to learn to identify lawsuits that disguise practices of legal intimidation under the cover of private legal disputes. SLAPPs that are not identified by the courts may never be counted. Efforts at grassroots education on SLAPPs carried out in the United States are thus aimed in large measure at giving citizens the necessary tools for the identification and management of strategic lawsuits against public participation.
2. In October 2011, these states included the following: Arizona, Louisiana, New York, Arkansas, Maine, Oklahoma, California, Maryland, Oregon, Delaware, Massachusetts, Colorado, Pennsylvania, Florida, Minnesota, Rhode Island, Georgia, Missouri, Tennessee, Texas, Hawaii, Nebraska, Utah, Illinois, Nevada, Washington, Indiana, Vermont and New Mexico. The territory of Guam also has an anti-SLAPP law. As this book was being written, steps were being taken by a coalition of American organizations to convince federal legislators to adopt an anti-SLAPP law applicable throughout the United States. See *The Public Participation Project* at <www.anti-slapp.org>.
3. This bill, entitled *The Citizen Participation Act of 2009* (H.R. 4364), has not yet, however, been passed into law. More details will be provided in the next chapter.

4. The American literature mainly concerns communications addressed to public authorities; the section below goes into greater detail on the constitutional and cultural factors that explain this focus.
5. SLAPPs frequently include, as the named parties, unidentified citizens ("John Does") who can eventually be included in the lawsuit. This technique is a very effective way to discourage the continuation of political activities by citizens still not targeted by the suit.
6. The confusion of the distinctions typically made between the concepts of private life and public life is a characteristic of SLAPP cases. We will see below how SLAPPs privatize the costs and risks associated with public participation. See McEvoy 1990.
7. Distinctions are made in the United States between SLAPPs taking place in the residential sector, those orchestrated by agencies of the government, those called "eco-SLAPPs," in the environmental sector, "not-in-my-backyard" SLAPPs resulting from opposition to the development of social (halfway houses, clinics for drug addicts) or economic projects (creating landfills or building factories) in residential communities, and SLAPPs launched to deny the exercise of specific rights (union rights, gender equality, freedom of expression). See Pring and Canan 1996.
8. Note: I do not wish to imply that the legal proceedings undertaken or considered by these people constitute SLAPPs. Readers will have to form their own opinions on the issue. These cases have, however, been associated publicly with the SLAPP issue in Quebec by various commentators.
9. This suit, brought by Jean Charest following public accusations made by his former Minister regarding possible collusion between the Liberal Party of Quebec and its fundraisers, is ironic in the sense that Bellemare used the anti-SLAPP legislation adopted under the government of his adversary. See Boivin 2010; Robitaille 2010; Agence QMI 2011.
10. See Fédération professionnelle des journalistes du Québec 2011; Société Radio-Canada 2011.
11. Beatty, however, makes the excellent point that being on the receiving end of such a suit can have the opposite effect on the targeted activists and galvanize public mobilization rather than stifling it. Various Quebec cases, which will be presented in Chapter 4, show the different impacts of such lawsuits on social mobilization (Beatty 1993).
12. According to Braun: "The entire character of public discourse is polluted when intimidation becomes a common or acceptable tactic. This intimidation, and the personal cost and psychic trauma to victims of the SLAPP technique, is itself a matter of concern, as is anything which deters citizens from public service and participation in government and public debates" (Braun 1999: 972).
13. This phenomenon is perceptible in Quebec. The journalists of the public affairs TV show *La Facture* on Radio-Canada have had to deal with the silence of many communities that have refused to speak on camera about alleged cases of SLAPPs out of fear of reprisals (see Société Radio-Canada 2006a, October 3).
14. *Gordon v. Marrone* 1992. Quoted by Lott 2004.
15. The permanent injunction, however, was not granted, in spite of ongoing efforts by the plaintiffs. See *Association québécoise de lutte contre la pollution atmosphérique (AQLPA) c. Compagnie américaine de fer et métaux inc. (AIM)*, 2006 QCCS 3949 (CanLII).
16. This is, for example, asserted by Abell, who thus summarizes the process of privatization of the issues associated with the public participation of citizens: "Suddenly, instead

17. Legal intimidation is a strategy deployed by a wide range of private and public actors who possess the resources required for the strategic use of legal disputes. This can be seen in particular in commercial disputes between parties with disproportionate resources.
18. Quebec is no exception; various initiatives, more or less satisfactory, have been established in order to remedy the relative lack of access to justice in Quebec (see Groupe de travail sur la révision du régime d'aide juridique au Québec 2005).
19. These unequal relationships allow, in certain cases, the plaintiff to include in these agreements "gag clauses" through which defendants agree not to comment in the future on the case originally under dispute (the very source of the social and political opposition that had induced them to express themselves publicly) and the terms of that agreement. The gag clauses contained in out-of-court settlements therefore amount to forced renunciation — although concealed under an appearance of voluntary consent — of political rights. This situation has, for example, occurred with one of the presumed SLAPP suits most widely covered ever in the media in Quebec, which will be discussed in Chapter 3. The signing of such agreements has been considered highly problematic by various actors in Quebec civil society, who see this as a direct attack on the freedom of expression of the defendant (see Ligue des droits et libertés 2008; see also AQLPA and CRRE 2008).
20. Interestingly enough, this guilty plea was made only a few moments before the judgment of the municipal court, thus preventing the reading of the initial judgment and forcing the judge to reconsider his decision in light of this new information. Ferti-Val explained this shift in approach by changes that had occurred in the management of the company.
21. This list is not intended to be exhaustive, but highlights the main legal concepts mobilized in relationship to public discussions on SLAPPs in Quebec and in Canada.
22. This being said, the Quebec *Charter of Human Rights and Freedoms*, which has quasi-constitutional authority, applies not only to relationships between the state and the citizens of Quebec, but also to those between private individuals.
23. Article 14 of the ICCPR protects the right to equal access to justice. It reads as follows: "All persons shall be equal before the courts and tribunals. In the determination of any criminal charge against him, or of his rights and obligations in a suit at law, everyone shall be entitled to a fair and public hearing by a competent, independent and impartial tribunal established by law."
24. The initiatives put in place include creation of the Small Claims Court and the creation of administrative tribunals (including the Régie du logement [Rental Board]) to streamline legal proceedings and reduce the costs associated with settling legal disputes.
25. With a personal contribution of $800, a single individual could get legal aid in 2011 if his or her annual income was less than $17,845. The annual income of a single person working full time at minimum wage in Quebec was then $20,072.
26. The Canadian Charter has been interpreted by the courts as a tool that is supposed to protect the citizens of the country from their governments and not as a set of norms to regulate the behaviour of citizens with each other.
27. The Human Rights Committee is under the auspices of the Office of the United

Nations High Commissioner for Human Rights and was established by article 28 of the *International Covenant on Civil and Political Rights*. Its mandate includes receiving and reviewing communications from citizens who say they have been victims of violations of the rights outlined in the Covenant as well as monitoring its application.

28. These points were presented and detailed in a written report by an expert panel that had been mandated by the Quebec government to study the problem of SLAPPs in Quebec. This committee also played a significant role in the affirmation of an anti-SLAPP movement in Quebec. This role is covered in detail in Chapter 4. See MacDonald et al. 2007. The contributions made by this expert panel to the debate on SLAPPs in Quebec will be presented and discussed in Chapter 4.

29. Quebec has similar legislation. See *An Act respecting access to documents held by public bodies and the Protection of personal information*, RSQ, chapter A-2.1.

Chapter 3

Legal Intimidation and Legislation
International and National Perspectives

The existence of strategic lawsuits against public participation has been observed in various countries that belong to common law legal traditions and has pushed citizens, lawyers and legislators to demand the adoption of legal provisions to counteract them.[1] Legislative measures have, for example, been introduced and sometimes brought into effect, in the United States, Australia and Canada. These laws frequently represent the outcome of long-term processes of social mobilization. However, not all have been equally effective. Some of these laws have been bold, containing proactive measures to prevent legal entanglements for SLAPP victims. Others, unfortunately, have not fulfilled their mandate.

This chapter presents a few of the various legislative avenues that have been considered or adopted by these states, provinces and territories and, briefly, the legal and legislative issues associated with the anti-SLAPP struggle.

On the whole, for any legislative measure to effectively counteract strategic lawsuits against public participation, it has to include four fundamental dimensions. One of these dimensions is *protective*; it has to ensure the protection of citizens participating in good faith in public debate. This can be done in two ways. First of all, by quickly putting a stop to requests to gag social and political opposition. It is important, above all, to avoid legal entanglements for the individuals and groups targeted by gag suits that appear to be potential SLAPPs. Second, the provision of financial protection is necessary for people or groups who have participated in public debate, so that they are not forced to sacrifice their financial security to defend themselves.

Effective anti-SLAPP legislation is also *dissuasive*; the objective is to create sufficient risk so that the potential SLAPPer will hesitate before using this practice of legal intimidation. This risk has the greatest effect when there is high probability in the courts of prompt dismissal and severe financial punishment for SLAPP instigators.

Third, anti-SLAPP mechanisms need to include a *restorative* dimension; they should make possible full and complete compensation (if possible) for moral, psychological and financial damages suffered by victims of legal intimidation. This compensation assumes finally, and this is essential, a *punishment* for the SLAPPer, which will be ordered to reimburse the expenses incurred by its adversary and to pay damages, including punitive damages.

The ways of including these four dimensions of protection, dissuasion, compensation and punishment in the legislative texts adopted to counteract SLAPPs depend on the political will of legislators to curb the phenomenon, the various regional and national legal cultures, and the general organization of the law that prevails within the different jurisdictions where these laws are adopted. American legislative experiments provide some relevant lessons on how to design responses to SLAPPs.

The United States on the Front Line

Short of a gun to the head, a greater threat to First Amendment expression can scarcely be imagined.— Judge Colabella, in *Gordon v. Marrone* 1992

The anti-SLAPP struggle in the United States is based on a paradox. On the one hand, American legal culture favours the swift use of litigation and the strategic use of the legal system in economic or political conflicts — in particular in order to contain social and political dissidence. On the other hand, this same legal culture formally recognizes civil and political rights as the apex of the constitutional apparatus of the country, with the express function of protecting the healthy conduct of public debates. This paradox, this apparent contradiction, perhaps explains the desire shown by American legislators to protect the citizens of the country against the undue judicialization of political debates. Certain legislative models adopted in the United States and presented below have, moreover, become international reference points on the subject.

Strategic lawsuits against public participation are essentially perceived in the United States as a serious threat to citizens' right to petition. This right is supposed to ensure healthy communication and exchange of information among citizens and public authorities.[2] The right to petition is protected by the first amendment of the American Constitution and occupies a key role in the organization of political life of that country.[3]

American anti-SLAPP legislation, as well as the constitutional and legal provisions intended to protect citizens from strategic lawsuits, do not seek so much to preserve healthy discussion of public affairs among citizens (that is more of a matter of the right to freedom of expression and the right to freedom of the press) than to keep open channels of communication between the citizens and their representatives. *SLAPPs thus appear in the United States as essentially a threat to representative democracy* (as opposed to, for example, being considered a threat to deliberative and participatory democracy in Canada) (see Tollefson 1994; Pring 1989). The right to petition is invoked not only in order to legitimize certain actions taken in the public sphere, but especially to justify the quick dismissal by the courts of lawsuits brought against citizens who have directly or indirectly petitioned their government.[4] The growing numbers of cases considered to be strategic lawsuits against public participation during the 1980s and 1990s became a constitutional issue in the United States, with the strategic instrumentalization of the legal system for the purposes of political gagging being perceived as a serious attack on the right to petition of American citizens (see, for example, Barker 1993; Jackson 2001; Kohler 2004; Stein 1989; Waldman 1993).

The question then consisted of determining the extent of the protection being offered by this right to citizens targeted by SLAPPs and the most effective ways for these citizens to take advantage of it. Three variables then came into play: the audience criterion, the definition of the act of petition and the definition of government. The American courts consequently had to establish first of all if communications indirectly addressed to legislators — and in particular those aimed at influencing public opinion, to attract the attention of the media or to express an opinion to a third party — were protected by the right to petition. This point is fundamental: a strict interpretation of the audience criterion associated with right to petition, not covering the communications addressed explicitly and directly to the government, would in practice exclude gestures, actions and communications aimed primarily at mobilizing public opinion or segments of the public. It would thus strip of constitutional protection the efforts addressed to the media or specific groups within civil society.

The American legal system then had to identify the activities arising from an authentic desire to transmit information of public interest to the powers that be (public demonstrations, sending letters and e-mails, lobbying, presentations in public and before administrative and legal bodies, picketing, etc.) or to influence these bodies. Not all public or legal activity conveys an authentic process of communication seeking to inform or influence the authorities; it seemed necessary to define the spectrum of citizen actions that could be considered authentic acts of petition.

Finally, the definition of what is understood by "government" proved to be a key factor: which actors and institutions could be included under this conceptual umbrella? It was a matter of establishing whether, and to what extent, communications addressed to the legislative, executive or judicial branches of the American government were protected by the constitutional right to petition. This process — identifying the audience of the communication and the activities that could be part of legitimate communication directed toward public authorities, as well as evaluating the scope given to the concept of government — made it possible to circumscribe the extent of the constitutional protection that could be claimed by potential victims of SLAPPs in the United States.

It is not necessary here to go into the subtleties of American jurisprudence; suffice it to mention that the right to petition has been the subject of a generous interpretation by the Supreme Court of the United States.[5] It now covers communications both directly and indirectly addressed to the government, a wide range of expressions and actions related to public communication, communications addressed to the various legislative, executive and legal branches of the different levels of government (local, regional, national), and all communications seeking to influence government. This right goes so far as to protect communications that are inaccurate, false or seek to lead the public and the government into error.

As a legal principle legitimizing both the quick dismissal of proceedings considered abusive or interfering with the right to petition of defendant parties and the financial penalization of SLAPPers, the right to petition already enjoyed a liberal interpretation from the American courts. The challenge was thus to introduce mechanisms to ensure the actual exercise of this right in relationship to lawsuits attempting to repress the individuals and groups using it.

This being said, the adoption of anti-SLAPP legislative measures has frequently been controversial. These measures commonly assume the implementation of procedures that are supposed to lead to or favour the quick termination of legal proceedings (interfering with the right of the plaintiff to bring a case to court) and the reorganization of legal proceedings so as to lighten the burden of the defendant while increasing that of the plaintiff. Not everyone agreed on the merits and necessity of a reorganization of legal procedures to favour the defendant.

In spite of these controversies, around thirty states wishing to protect the right to petition of their citizens have so far established legislative models to prevent the abusive political instrumentalization of the legal system and penalize the instigators of such proceedings. Since the quality of these various anti-SLAPP mechanisms vary greatly, Professors George W. Pring and Penelope Canan (whose work has strongly influenced and legitimized the legislative changes made in many of these jurisdictions) have defined three criteria on the basis of which to evaluate the quality of the legislative provisions adopted in the United States. They must pass three tests:

1. **Communications:** The legislation must cover all communications to government, whether direct or indirect and whether in the form of testimony, letters, peaceful demonstrations, petitions to government, etc.
2. **Forums:** The protections offered by the legislation adopted must cover all government bodies and agents, whether federal, state, or local, and whether legislative, executive, judicial, or the electorate.
3. **Prevention and Cure:** The legislation adopted must set out an effective early review for filed SLAPPs, shifting the burden of proof to the filer and, in so doing, serving a clear warning against the future filing of such suits. (Pring and Canan 1996: 189)

The significance of the anti-SLAPP legislation that has been adopted in the United States therefore varies according to the criteria of access to the protections offered, the quality and extent of those protections, the dissuasive force of the provisions and their ability to compensate for the moral and financial damage suffered by the victims. Since there have been too many anti-SLAPP laws adopted for us to be able to examine them all in detail, the following section is limited to two particular state laws as well as a recent federal bill that died on the order paper. In addition to illustrating a real will to fight the phenomenon, these legislative models propose mechanisms that are particularly interesting to meet the objectives of protection, dissuasion, compensation and punishment mentioned above.

The Minnesota Law

In 1994, Minnesota tabled an anti-SLAPP bill confirming both the legal priority of the right to petition (unusually presented under the concept of "public participation"[6]) and the central character of this concept in the organization of the democratic life of the government. The legal mechanism proposed by the Minnesota law is aimed at the quick dismissal of lawsuits that interfere unduly with the public participation of the defendant, recovery of the legal costs incurred by the defendant (including the lawyer's fees) and financial penalties for the instigator of a suit that has the purpose of limiting the exercise of the constitutional rights of a citizen. The process used to accomplish this consists essentially of granting immunity for any act of public participation, as long as it does not violate the constitutional rights of another party.[7]

By virtue of this legislation, a party that is the subject of legal proceedings can make a motion for dismissal to the court, alleging that the proceedings undertaken against him or her are the result of an act of public participation protected under this law. The usual legal procedures (and in particular requests for information from the opposing party) are immediately suspended until the motion to dismiss has been heard and ruled on (Minnesota, section 554.02. (1)). The party that instigated the proceedings is then obliged to present "clear and convincing evidence" to the court to show that the act of its adversary, for which the latter is the subject of the legal proceedings, is not immunized under section 554.03 (see above). The failure to demonstrate this results in automatic dismissal of the claim and reimbursement of the legal expenses incurred by the responding party (sections 554.02 (3) and 554.04).

The responding party who has obtained dismissal of the proceedings instituted against him or her according to the provisions contained in this law will be able to obtain payment of additional damages if he or she is able to show a court that the responding party (the original plaintiff) brought the suit against him or her for the purpose of harassment, to inhibit his or her public participation, to interfere with the exercise of his or her constitutional rights or to otherwise wrongfully injure the moving party (section 554.04(b)).

This legislation thus affirms the preponderance of a moral and legal principle based on free and open discussion among public authorities and the electorate. This principle cuts short legal claims that are not based on a violation of the constitutional rights of the party introducing the proceedings. It is not therefore a matter of rebalancing a set of rights that come into conflict through citizen participation in public debate — that is, for example, the case for the Quebec anti-SLAPP legislation[8] — than to affirm the primacy of a principle of political participation over rights with lower precedence.[9]

It should be noted that the law adopted in Minnesota failed to establish a specific procedure to ensure the prompt dismissal of strategic lawsuits against public participation. The suspension of the usual proceedings and the reversal of the burden of proof in favour of the defendant should be enough to speed up dismissal. However, certain commentators maintain that many American anti-SLAPP laws have been failures, empty shells that reaffirm principles of consensual political participation but that are incapable of effectively and promptly disposing of abusive lawsuits (see Cohen 2010, July 23). The California law proposes an answer to the problem of cases dragging on by establishing an accelerated procedure for cases that appear to be strategic lawsuits against public participation.

The California Law

The California anti-SLAPP law, adopted in 1992 and amended several times (in particular to prevent its improper use[10]), is certainly one of the measures that has received the most attention internationally. It is still widely considered a reference on the subject.[11] Section 425.16 of the California Code of Civil Procedure stipulates in its introduction:

> The Legislature finds and declares that there has been a disturbing increase in lawsuits brought primarily to chill the valid exercise of the constitutional rights of freedom of speech and petition for the redress of grievances. The Legislature finds and declares that it is in the public interest to encourage continued participation in matters of public significance, and that this participation should not be chilled through abuse of the judicial process. To this end, this section shall be construed broadly. (section 425.16 (a))

The anti-SLAPP provisions adopted in California apply in cases involving the right to petition or the freedom of expression of a person with respect to an issue of public interest. Defendants who wish to take advantage of the provisions of the law have to show the court that the lawsuit instituted against them interferes with their right to petition or their right to freedom of expression, which they have exercised during a controversy, a communication or a discussion related to an issue of public interest.[12] The protection offered by the California law covers a range of communications and includes discussions of public interest addressing only indirectly public institutions and agents. It protects:

> 1. Any written or oral statement or writing made before a legislative, executive, or judicial proceeding, or any other official proceeding authorized by law;

2. Any written or oral statement or writing made in connection with an issue under consideration or review by a legislative, executive, or judicial body, or any other official proceeding authorized by law;
3. Any written or oral statement or writing made in a place open to the public or a public forum in connection with an issue of public interest; or,
4. Any other conduct in furtherance of the exercise of the constitutional right to petition or the constitutional right of free speech in connection with a public issue or an issue of public interest. (section 3 (e))

The California law includes specific provisions that are worth studying. It permits first of all the rapid quashing of strategic lawsuits against public participation through an emergency procedure that ensures the quick hearing of the case by a qualified court. The defendant has 60 days following the filing of the action (or more, if the court allows it) to file a motion to strike (section (2)(f)). This request will then be heard and considered within 30 days. Then there is a reversal of the burden of proof, with the plaintiff obliged to convince the court that there is a probability that it will win the cause at trial. This demonstration is complicated by the extent of the protection given to freedom of expression and the right to petition on American soil.[13] All the legal proceedings associated with the initial lawsuit are suspended until the court rules regarding dismissal of the lawsuit.

This procedure, exceptionally rapid, seeks to avoid entanglements for citizens who have exercised their right to petition in a slow and overly onerous legal system. The motion to dismiss will be accepted if: 1) the defendant has been able to demonstrate that the lawsuit arises from the exercise of his or her right to petition or interferes with this right; and 2) the plaintiff has not been able to demonstrate the existence of a probability that it will win the case against the defendant.[14]

The defendant who is granted a motion to dismiss will then be able to recover legal and extralegal costs (including attorney's fees) and will be able, if he or she so desires and considers it appropriate, to sue the party that brought the original suit for damages.[15] This process, called "SLAPPback" by the California legislation, is intended as proceedings for compensation specifically devoted to the protection of the right to freedom of expression and petition of the citizens of California:

> The Legislature finds and declares that a SLAPPback is distinguishable in character and origin from the ordinary malicious prosecution action. The Legislature further finds and declares that a SLAPPback cause of action should be treated differently, as provided in this section, from an ordinary malicious prosecution action because a SLAPPback is consistent with the Legislature's intent to protect the valid exercise of the constitutional rights of free speech and petition by its deterrent effect on SLAPP (strategic lawsuits against public participation) litigation and by its restoration of public confidence in participatory democracy. (section 425.18. (a))

This specific procedure is aimed at both dissuading potential instigators of such lawsuits from using legal intimidation to muzzle opponents — the damages awarded to victims of abusive lawsuits can be substantial — and to ensure compensation for the psychological, economic, family and moral damages caused by the initial lawsuit.

A Federal Bill

At the same time as legislative changes are being made in several states, various civil society groups have called for the adoption of national anti-SLAPP legislation. These efforts had an initial, fragile success with the introduction in December 2009 of a bill to the American Congress. Entitled *Citizen Participation Act of 2009* (H.R. 4364), the bill was supposed to standardize and extend protection against SLAPPs to all American citizens. It died on the order paper, however, since it was not passed within the time limit prescribed by the session of Congress. Nevertheless it commonly happens that bills are revived by members of Congress in subsequent sessions. For the proponents of federal anti-SLAPP legislation, the question then becomes one of strengthening social and political consensus around the issue and obtaining the support of politicians who can champion the legislative initiative in the face of the resistance encountered. Various American groups are currently mobilizing to get the federal legislation adopted.[16]

The legislative uniformization proposed by the *Citizen Participation Act* is based, unsurprisingly, on moral and political considerations: it seems unjust that certain citizens enjoy protection from the abusive judicialization of social and political controversies while others are denied it. The proposal also has a strategic purpose: the adoption of national legislation is supposed to counteract what is called in the English-language literature *forum shopping* — the selection, by the SLAPPers, of state jurisdictions where it is the easiest and safest to sue their adversaries. This situation is exacerbated by the increasing use (and the attendant legal repression) of technologies and media that seem to have limitless possibilities. The legal repression of bloggers and citizen journalists (called cyber-SLAPPs) is frequently accompanied by a careful selection of the jurisdiction in which the suit is instigated (see Furman 2001).

The *Citizen Participation Act* was supposed to provide immunity to all acts of petition, as long as they were carried out in a non-malicious manner.[17] Interestingly, the procedural protections (and in particular the rapid quashing of the legal action, the reversal of the burden of proof and the organization of an expedited process) offered by the bill would be applied to both suits infringing on the right to petition and suits infringing on free speech (section 4 of the bill).

The mechanism proposed is based on the following steps: movement of cases to federal courts; expedited hearing and dismissal of cases; reversal of the burden of proof; reimbursement of legal costs incurred; and compensation for SLAPP victims. If it were adopted, this bill would permit all individuals who feel that a civil suit instituted against them before a state court is aimed at an immunized activity or the exercise of their constitutional right to petition or freedom of expression to request the removal of this legal action to a district court of the United States (section 6 (a)). This move would ensure, in practice, the standardization of the protection offered in all the states of the Union.[18]

Defendants could then file a special motion to dismiss against any claim resulting from an action that they considered immunized or related to their constitutional right to petition or freedom of expression. They would then have to provide the court with *prima facie* evidence that the legal action arises from the exercise of their constitutional rights (section 5(b)). Once this requirement is met, the court would then reverse the burden of proof and require the plaintiff to show both the legal foundation of the case and demonstrate *prima facie* the facts that are likely to give him or her a favourable verdict. The failure of such a demonstration would lead to dismissal of the suit.

The filing of a motion to dismiss would suspend discovery proceedings against the opposing party until the court makes a decision (or until the court orders, with justifications, that the discovery proceedings will proceed) (section 5 (c)). The court would hold hearings on the motion to dismiss and render its verdict as soon as possible. It would have to justify its denial of the motion to dismiss. The defendant would retain the right to appeal such a denial (section 5 (e)).

In addition, the bill tries to protect the anonymity of people who have exercised their constitutional rights of petition or freedom of expression. It would thus be possible for the defendant to file a motion to quash aimed at dismissing or declaring invalid proceedings or discovery proceedings that identify individuals or groups requesting anonymity.[19]

Adoption of a motion to dismiss the claim, the proceedings or the discovery proceedings identifying individuals or groups requesting anonymity would lead to reimbursement of legal costs, including lawyer's fees (section 8 (a)). Quite exceptionally, this bill proposes forbidding a party whose legal action has been dismissed under its provisions from declaring bankruptcy (which would allow it to avoid reimbursement of the costs incurred by its adversary). This procedure is extended to the reimbursement of the damages claimed by SLAPP victims in state jurisdictions (section 9).

The United States is certainly the epicentre of the problem of intimidation and legal repression. Some states have decided to act; others hesitate to do so. The *Citizen Participation Act*, the first attempt at federal anti-SLAPP legislative, was introduced by Congressman Steve Cohen in late 2009. The future of the initiative is uncertain at this time.

The Australian Case

Australia has a history of legislative failures that will nevertheless help us to better define SLAPPs and understand how to fight them. The Australian non-profit sector, and more specifically citizens and groups active on environmental issues, have been for many years dealing with the multiplication of lawsuits that have been frequently considered strategic lawsuits against public participation.

This trend toward legal intimidation seems to be now firmly established in Australia. The Gunns case is still certainly the legal case that has contributed the most in recent years to publicizing the legal repression of social and political activism. On December 13, 2004, the Gunns timber company, one of the biggest forestry firms operating in Australia, initiated legal proceedings against seventeen individuals and three community groups who were opposing clearcutting in Tasmania (see *Gunns Limited v. Marr*, VSC 251, 2005; <www.austlii.edu.au/au/cases/vic/VSC/2005/251.html>). These groups and individuals, later nicknamed the Gunns 20, were then accused not only of defamation — a common allegation in SLAPP cases — but also (among other things) of mischief, trespass and interference with the business interests of the company.[20] The activists were sued for more than 6.4 million dollars. The case dragged on for more than five years and ended in January 2010 with the forestry company dropping the charges against the last four opponents targeted by the suit (settlements and dropped charges had gradually reduced the number of defendants). Gunns also reimbursed substantial amounts of legal costs incurred by its adversaries (see the following articles on the Gunns 20 case: Rickarby 2010; Glaetzer 2010).

The Gunns 20 suit is not an isolated case. The problem was considered so serious that more than 140 Australian lawyers signed an open letter in 2006 asking Australian legislators to make reforms to protect the right to public participation of citizens.

> As senior lawyers practising, advising and writing in the area of the law of public interest debate, we call on all Australian governments to implement law reform to protect the community's right and ability to participate in public debate and political activity without fear of litigation.
>
> The increasing phenomenon of litigation against community participation in public affairs by comment or action has the serious effect of intimidating the community, chilling public debate and silencing voices which should be heard in a democratic society. In addition these lawsuits against public participation create enormous stress and financial burden for the people and groups who are sued and clog our court systems with arguments which belong in political rather than legal arenas.
>
> Free speech and robust public debate, together with the ability to participate in community and political activity without fear of litigation, are fundamental rights in a democratic society. The increasing and wide-

spread use of defamation law, trade practices laws and economic torts laws against public participation must be wound back. It is no coincidence that societies where these rights of public participation are curtailed have historically been burdened with corruption, inefficiency and often disastrous decision making.

Legislation specifically to protect the community's right to public debate and participation has been introduced in 25 jurisdictions in the United States. We call on Australian governments to introduce similar laws and work together to achieve national or uniform legislation in Australia.[21]

The Australian legal context differs significantly from the Canadian and American contexts to the extent that there is no constitutional mechanism that explicitly confirms the fundamental rights that form the basis for a way to counteract SLAPPs. Australia does not, in fact, have any charter, constitution or declaration explicitly defining the rights and freedoms of the citizens of the country.[22]

In the absence of clear national legislation providing guidelines on the basis of which SLAPPs can be dismissed, Australian stakeholders concerned about the phenomenon have essentially proposed two distinct, although complementary, reforms.

The first of these reforms was supposed to harmonize the legal provisions related to defamation for the entire country. The different states and territories of Australia had, in fact, at the time the reform came into effect in January 2006, made specific provisions in this area. This lack of uniformity previous to the reform complicated legal proceedings considerably. The relevance of such a process therefore goes beyond the framework of strategic lawsuits against public participation, although its adoption is part of a broader process aimed at preventing the legal penalization of citizen activism. This reform had in particular the objective of ensuring:

> That the law of defamation does not place unreasonable limits on freedom of expression and, in particular, on the publication and discussion of matters of public interest and importance.[23]

One of the most sensitive points of this reform is certainly the removal of the right of corporations to initiate defamation proceedings. This bold measure, which is distinguished from the more moderate American and Canadian approaches, is clearly in keeping with a desire to rebalance social and legal forces. The reform is rooted in a reflection on the political instrumentalization of the right to reputation by corporations in order to gag criticism by citizens. Thus, in theory, it was supposed to contribute to defusing attempts at judicial intimidation and repression undertaken by legal persons mobilizing substantial legal capital in order to crush adversaries lacking such capital.

The applications of this reform are, however, limited in their scope. Companies with fewer than ten employees, as well as non-profit corporations, retain the right to initiate defamation proceedings. In addition, the administrators of corporations (as well as physical persons associated with them) retain the right to sue their alleged slanderers personally.

Even more importantly, while it should be acknowledged that this reform limits the repertoire of legal actions that can be deployed by corporations in order to gag political adversaries, it is necessary to specify that they still have at their disposal a wide range of legal means to do this. Commercial law offers corporations that want to use strategies of legal intimidation a wide range of legal avenues (interference with contractual business, unfair competition, unjustified financial and commercial losses, conspiracy, etc.) that permit them to impose their will on opponents or detractors.[24]

The Australian initiative thus favours, although in a partial and incomplete way, citizen criticism of commercial entities operating on the national territory. Along with this reform, certain Australian states and territories have — without much success — tried to adopt specific legislation to protect citizen participation in public debates.

The Tasmanian Bill

One of the most interesting anti-SLAPP bills was introduced without success in the Tasmanian House of Assembly in March 2005. The Tasmanian initiative illustrates the fascinating phenomenon of legislative imitation, since the legislation repeated almost all the mechanisms and vocabulary developed four years earlier in British Columbia. This bill, however, expanded significantly the scope of the protection offered by proposing a radical reform in the area of defamation.[25]

This bill proposed to, in particular:

1. Provide *qualified privilege* for communication or conduct that constitutes public participation;
2. Take away the right of corporations and any individual associated with a corporation to sue for defamation;
3. Take away the right by any politician to sue for defamation arising from statements relating to his or her conduct in office, as well as, in the absence of malice, on his or her fitness for office;
4. To make impossible the awarding of financial compensation resulting from *general damages* for defamation, in the absence of malice.[26]

This addition certainly made the Tasmanian legislative initiative one of the strongest bills in the world drafted to counteract strategic lawsuits against public participation. Its focus on questions associated with defamation expresses a social and political concern regarding the instrumentalization of the right to reputation in Tasmania for the purposes of the judicial gagging of citizen expression.

The Tasmanian bill, entitled *Protection of Public Participation Bill 2005*,[27] had the objectives of protecting citizen participation in public debate and dissuading both physical persons and legal persons from undertaking improper legal proceedings. To accomplish this, it was based on the legislative mechanisms developed in British Columbia,[28] discussed below in this chapter.

Although it was vigorously defended by the Green Party, this bill never became a legislative priority of the government. No substantial legislative action was taken to permit its adoption.[29]

South Australia

Three bills have been introduced successively and without success in the House of Assembly of South Australia since 2005 to counteract the strategic lawsuits against public participation and protect public participation in that state.[30] The most recent one, introduced in first reading in February 2008, essentially repeated the objectives of protection, compensation and dissuasion contained in the Tasmanian legislative initiative. There were, however, significant differences in the mechanisms and definitions used.

The South Australia bill seems at first glance to be more modest in scope than its Tasmanian counterpart: it avoided, in fact, proposing any major reforms to defamation law.[31] It nevertheless proposed some interesting initiatives. It defined a right to public participation, thus establishing a clear legislative standard on the basis of which the dismissal of abusive suits could be favoured.[32] The exercise of this right was supposed to be favoured by various strategies applied upstream, in the courts, and downstream with legal proceedings.

A person targeted by the threat of a suit could apply to the Magistrates Court for a declaration stating that the communications or conduct that they have undertaken (and for which legal proceedings have been instituted against him or her) constituted public participation and that, consequently, the proceedings against him or her would be inconsistent with the exercise of the right to public participation (section 6). This procedure was supposed to counteract the process of judicial intimidation by permitting the defendant to obtain both a preliminary legal opinion confirming the legitimate nature of the acts that he or she is being sued for, and warning the potential intimidator that subsequent legal action is likely to be judged illegitimate by the courts. The bill also included provisions to suspend the legal proceedings instigated against the defendant until the court has ruled on the abusive or legitimate nature of the legal action instituted against the defendant (section 7 (3)).

The South Australia anti-SLAPP bill proposed a significant reduction of the burden placed on the potential victim while avoiding associated processes for the dismissal of proceedings and recovery of costs generated by the suit with *intentions* of the plaintiff. The model developed focused instead on the *effects* of potentially abusive lawsuits on the right of the defendant to public participation. This point is fundamental: the mechanism proposed here was aimed at prompt dismissal of gag suits — proceedings that have the effect of preventing and limiting public debate — and the penalization of proceedings that appear to be strategic lawsuits against public participation (in this case, the proceedings instigated for the purpose of gagging or intimidating political adversaries). This approach is certainly promising. It remains, in fact, much easier to show the negative effects of a lawsuit on the public participation of citizens targeted by it than to demonstrate the intentions of its instigator in front of a court.

It should be noted that it is not a question here for the defendant of proving the veracity or exactitude of public communications or conduct, but rather for the court of deciding both on his or her good faith and the "reasonable" nature of the actions or words of the defendant. This mechanism was thus intended to protect the conduct, communications and actions that could have been prejudicial, although carried out in good faith in relationship to public participation (section 7(4)). Despite its promise, the bill did not get past the stage of the first reading in the House.

Australian Capital Territory

The Australian Capital Territory adopted in September 2008 the first (and so far only) Australian anti-SLAPP law. This law, entitled *Protection of Public Participation Act*, is the most modest legislative model of the examples presented in this section. Beyond the signal that it sends regarding the desire of the legislator to protect public debate, it is generally not of much interest.

This legislation seeks to protect public participation and discourages the instigation of proceedings that a "reasonable person would consider interfere with engagement in public participation."[33] This criterion is contained in the very definition of the concept of public participation established by this legislation:

> Public participation means conduct that a reasonable person would consider is intended (in whole or part) to influence public opinion, or promote further action by the public, a corporation or government entity in relation to an issue of public interest. (section 7(1))

A legal proceeding will be considered illegitimate if the court establishes that a reasonable person would agree that this action was instigated in order to discourage the defendant (or any other person) from engaging publicly, to divert the defendant's resources away from engagement to the proceeding or to punish him or her for engaging in public participation (section 6).

One important fact: the law adopted by the Australian Capital Territory does not apply to cases of defamation, although these constitute a substantial proportion of the lawsuits instituted against citizens who have participated in public debate in Australia (see Walters 2003). In addition, this legislation gives the court the power to condemn the party that instigated illegitimate legal action following public participation by the defendant to pay a financial penalty to the Capital Territory. This financial penalty is intended to be strictly dissuasive and not to compensate in any way for financial and psychological damages suffered by the victim of the SLAPP. No mechanism for the quick dismissal of lawsuits that interfere with public participation of the citizens of the Territory was established by this law.

The Canadian Case

Strategic lawsuits against public participation as a phenomenon of legal intimidation have been observed since the early 1990s in Canada.[34] The first recorded SLAPP cases seem to have appeared on the west coast of the country, mostly in British Columbia, and were mainly related to environmental or residential conflicts. I will briefly present here a few cases that have been publicly referred to as SLAPPs or that are closely associated with this concept before going into more detail on the legal and legislative issues related to the Canadian context.

SLAPPs: Two Key Canadian Cases

Daishowa Inc. v. Friends of the Lubicon

The *Daishowa v. Friends of the Lubicon* case had considerable resonance in English Canada during the 1990s and focused attention on an increasing problem of judicial repression of citizen activism. This conflict, which took a constitutional turn, opposed the Japanese paper company Daishowa Inc. and a non-profit association working to defend the rights of the Lubicon Cree community. The non-government organization maintained, like the Cree, that the paper company should refrain from all tree cutting in disputed territory of the Aboriginal community until the land claim was settled. Since the paper company refused to suspend its activities, the Friends of the Lubicon organized a national — and then international — boycott of the company's products.

In 1995 Daishowa initiated a defamation suit against the Friends of the Lubicon, alleging that it had suffered unjustified economic damage, including interference with its economic interests, intimidation, threats, interference with contractual relationships and conspiracy.[35] Daishowa was also contesting "secondary picketing" directed not against the company itself, but against its customers. In fact, members or sympathizers of the Friends of the Lubicon put pressure on companies that continued to buy Daishowa products in spite of the boycott, including by picketing.

The Ontario Court of Justice accepted of Daishowa's defamation claim, but awarded the company only one dollar in damages.[36] It confirmed the right of citizens to organize the peaceful boycott of the products of a private company, as well as the right to demonstrate in front of shopping centres where its products were sold.[37] The allegations of economic damage were rejected. The company appealed the verdict before negotiating an out-of-court settlement with its adversaries in May 2000, nine years after the beginning of the boycott and five years after the beginning of legal proceedings.[38] This case highlighted the difficulties — both financial and legal — faced by citizen organizations that possess limited means when conflicts are moved from a political arena to a legal arena by a party with much greater legal capital.[39]

Fraser v. Saanich

The British Columbia bench established a precedent in the history of Canadian jurisprudence on SLAPPs by using the term formally for the first time. The ruling given on May 31, 1999, on the case of *Fraser v. Saanich* marked the Canadian legal landscape both by defining a SLAPP legally and by penalizing the instigator of the proceedings.

The *Fraser v. Saanich* case followed a suit filed by the owner of a hospital building against citizens protesting the remodeling and sale of the building. The citizens, who were opposed to an enlargement of the building while it was in operation, requested a zoning change and designation of the building as a heritage site at the end of its operations in order to preserve its architectural and historical dimensions and to avoid the development of a large-scale complex in a residential area.[40] The change in zoning was eventually made, limiting the sales potential of the building. The owner brought lawsuits against the citizens who had demonstrated in this matter, as well as against the city of Saanich, alleging that there had been interference with contractual business, conspiracy, collusion, negligence and bad faith from the defendants (see Lott 2004).

In his verdict, Judge Singh declared the following:

> While neighbourhood participation in municipal politics often places an almost adversarial atmosphere into land use questions, this participation is a key element to the democratic involvement of said citizens in community decision making. Signing petitions, making submissions to municipal councils and even the organization of community action groups are sometimes the only avenues for community residents to express their views on land use issues. The solicitation of public opinion is specifically mandated in the Municipal Act. This type of activity often produces unfavourable results for some parties involved. However, an unfavourable action by local government does not, in the absence of some other wrongdoing, open the doors to seek redress on those who spoke out in favour of that action. To do so would place a chilling effect on the public's participation in local government.
>
> A SLAPP suit is a claim for monetary damages against individuals who have dealt with a government body on an issue of public interest or concern. It is a meritless action filed by a plaintiff whose primary goal is not to win the case but rather to silence or intimidate citizens who have participated in proceedings regarding public policy or public decision making.

What the plaintiffs expect to receive they should clearly also expect to deliver. I find, therefore, finally, that this action not only contains an unreasonable claim, is meritless and devoid of any factual foundation, but also has been used as an attempt to stifle the democratic activities of the defendants, the neighbourhood residents. I find the plaintiffs' conduct reprehensible and deserving of censure by an award of special costs. (*Fraser v. Saanich*)

Formal recognition by a British Columbia court of the existence of a strategy of political instrumentalization of the legal apparatus in order to gag social and political opposition led to beginnings of discussion on the effectiveness of existing provisions to curb the phenomenon. This assessment is based essentially on three different aspects:

1. Analysis of the constitutional protections offered by the Canadian *Charter of Rights and Freedoms*;
2. Analysis of the procedural protections existing in the *common law* provinces; and finally,
3. Evaluation of the merits of developing legislation specifically intended to eradicate SLAPPs.

SLAPP: Constitutional Protections

As seen above, discussions on strategic lawsuits against public participation has revolved mainly, in the United States, around the concept of the right to petition, a fundamental constitutional principle in the American system. The concept of the right to petition is, however, non-existent in the Canadian constitutional landscape, which substitutes the concept of freedom of expression.[41] The entrenchment of the Canadian *Charter of Rights and Freedoms* in the 1982 Constitution made freedom of expression a fundamental legal principle in Canada. The Charter, the cornerstone of a rights culture now imposed on the country, is, however, applied much more restrictively than the protections granted to American citizens by the Constitution of the United States. The Charter, in fact, applies only to the following institutions and actors:

   a) To the Parliament and government of Canada in respect of all matters within the authority of Parliament including all matters relating to the Yukon Territory and Northwest Territories; and
   b) To the legislature and government of each province in respect of all matters within the authority of the legislature of each province. (section 32.1)

Section 32.1 has been interpreted by the courts as providing a protection that Canadian citizens can claim to escape authoritarian abuses by Canadian public authorities, but also as a guideline that can be used to restrict the application of the Charter to government activities and actors only. Any legal claim using the Charter must therefore demonstrate some kind of participation by public authorities or actors covered by the Charter. It follows from this that the Canadian *Charter of Rights and Freedoms* is not applicable in legal disputes opposing strictly private parties.[42]

Since SLAPPs are civil lawsuits essentially (although not always) opposing private parties, it is doubtful that the constitutional protection of freedom of expression in Canada can be of any application to fight against them.[43] When SLAPPs occur, the question then becomes how to determine if the appeals to freedom of expression launched by the victims of these improper proceedings will be reflected in legal interpretations of the concept currently in effect. It is a matter of converging a moral principle and its legal interpretations.[44]

There is, to my knowledge, no jurisprudence providing a defence in the area of SLAPP based on the constitutional protection of freedom of expression that has been heard by the Supreme Court of Canada. The feasibility of such a process remains to be proven. The cumbersome nature of this process, as well as the level of legal uncertainty that is associated with it, has prompted various commentators to call for a process of legislative review at the provincial level.[45]

Such a legislative review, however, would have to be preceded by an evaluation of the protections offered in the common law provinces. It is therefore appropriate to evaluate whether the measures aimed at counteracting illegitimate lawsuits now included in procedural law could satisfactorily solve the problem of the strategic instrumentalization of the legal system embodied by SLAPPs.

Existing Procedural Protections in the Common Law Provinces

SLAPPs, as we saw in Chapter 1, constitute essentially an instrumentalization of legal proceedings to exhaust and demoralize a political adversary now confined to the legal arena.

The different Canadian territories and provinces that have a common law regime have thus put in place mechanisms to protect their citizens from "frivolous" (without legal foundation), "quarrelsome" (judicial harassment marked by increasing numbers of proceedings) or "vexatious" (harassment and oppression through legal avenues) legal proceedings (Pelletier 2008; Perell 2007). The legal regimes in place in the common law provinces thus grant a certain power to the courts to ensure the smooth operation of the hearings and prevent the abuse of proceedings. These powers allow, for example, the courts to grant a summary verdict by notice of motion, thus cutting short improper legal proceedings, but also to quash a legal action considered abusive and penalize the party that instigated it.

Mechanisms therefore exist and should theoretically permit both the quick dismissal of strategic lawsuits against public participation and the legal penalization of parties that have introduced improper claims. However, many commentators have noted the ineffectiveness of these measures in counteracting these lawsuits in Canada and recommend the drafting of legislation specifically to counteract them (for example, see Tollefson 1996; Pelletier 2008). There are essentially two reasons for this: first of all, the provisions currently included in common law are aimed at preventing abuses of the justice system in the broad sense and do not explicitly seek to counteract attempts at instrumentalizing the legal apparatus as a weapon of political oppression. They are therefore of limited use in situations where this is done rather subtly.

Second, and this is important, these provisions are out of step with a legal culture that does not favour the quick dismissal of potentially abusive proceedings. Pelletier (2008: 4) points out, for example:

> While some examples exist of the courts exercising these powers, they seem outnumbered by those in which the courts express their reluctance to deprive a plaintiff of an opportunity to prove his, her or its case in court after a full hearing on the merits. Thus, the power to dismiss a case as frivolous or vexatious or as an abuse of process is exercised only in the clearest of cases.

This overcautiousness of the courts in giving defendants quick dismissals of potentially abusive suits can be explained essentially by the fact that such a dismissal could be seen as a threat to the fundamental rights of the party that had introduced the proceedings. The right to go to court and be heard is a cornerstone of liberal democracy. Refusing a plaintiff the right to heard by a court is considered in the current legal culture to be a severe measure that must have a solid foundation. However, it is extremely difficult to demonstrate at the beginning of the hearing that a legal case that appears potentially to be a SLAPP *is* actually abusive (and not only that it *can* constitute an abuse of justice). In the absence of such a demonstration, it is probable that the court will refuse to deprive the plaintiff of its right to be heard. Pelletier (2008: 8), once again, is enlightening on this point:

> While the common law provides theoretical remedies for abuse of process, in the inherent jurisdiction of the courts, in the court statutes and rules, and in the law of tort, the practical application of these remedies provides small comfort to those being sued by strategic litigation and other persons the plaintiff wishes to intimidate. Either a way must be found to overcome the reluctance of courts to characterize such suits as abusive at early stages, or other remedies must be created for the harm these suits cause.

This is the heart of the problem. Although understandable, this caution encourages the prolongation of cases that could prove to be problematic. The anti-SLAPP legislative models considered or adopted in English Canada (detailed below) therefore had to send a message to the judiciary, telling it to take more stringent measures to deal with cases that have the appearance of abuse and to better balance the preservation of the right to go to court and the right to freedom of expression and public participation.

The alleged inability of procedural rules governing legal disputes to quickly dismiss SLAPPs, as well as the limitations of the constitutional protections provided by the Canadian *Charter of Rights and Freedoms*, have encouraged the development of various legislative approaches in the common law regimes of the country. These initiatives, so far inconclusive, do, however, represent attempts to deal with this problem.

Legislative Measures Taken in the Common Law Provinces

The visibility of certain alleged SLAPP cases in English Canada have highlighted the strategic and abusive use of the courts for political purposes in Canada over the last twenty years. Various legislative initiatives have been taken in British Columbia, Nova Scotia and New Brunswick to curtail the phenomenon. Currently, Ontario is considering following suit and adopting a law.

The British Columbia Law

The anti-SLAPP experience in British Columbia is one of a missed opportunity. British Columbia can pride itself in being the first Canadian province to have adopted an anti-SLAPP law. However, with a change of government, it was quickly repealed, putting an abrupt end to a rather promising legislative experiment.

Following repeated requests from community groups in the province, the Legislative Assembly of British Columbia adopted in April 2001 a law establishing the basis for legal protection of public participation from lawsuits with "improper purposes."[46] Entitled *The Protection of Public Participation Act*, this legislative initiative was intended to contribute to the quick dismissal of proceedings with improper purposes, permit the reimbursement of costs incurred unjustly by the defendant and award punitive damages to discourage this practice.[47] The legal mechanism established to accomplish this was based on several Canadian and foreign bills.[48]

A defendant who considers him- or herself a victim of a legal proceeding or claim for an improper purpose following public participation may apply to the court in the 60 days following reception of the proceedings against him or her and fewer than 120 days before the date scheduled for the hearing of the proceeding, for one or more of the following orders:

1. To dismiss the proceeding or claim;
2. For reasonable costs and expenses;
3. For punitive or exemplary damages against the plaintiff. (section 4(1))

This application would suspend all proceedings and applications related to the action against the defendant until the motion to dismiss has been heard and decided by the court (or at a previous time, if the court so rules) (section 4(2)(b)). This suspension of legal proceedings was intended to keep defendants from becoming entangled in tedious legal proceedings — out-of-court examinations and outrageous requests for documents by the opposing party, for example — in order to exhaust them or divert them from their political actions. It was thus a matter of the defendants alleging that the *motives* behind the action against them were illegitimate in order to implement a mechanism permitting the quick dismissal of the action, and the legal and financial penalization of the party that had brought it.

This legislation also stipulated a change in the legal provisions on defamation. It gave qualified privilege to "communication or conduct that constitutes the public participation" (section 3). This immunity was intended to protect actions and communications that, although they could be prejudicial, had been carried out in good faith. It forced the party wanting to bring a defamation suit against a person participating in a public debate to demonstrate the existence of malicious intentions on the part of its adversary.

The main weakness of this legislation lay in the selection of the criteria defining an action or proceeding that hid illegitimate intentions. In order to authorize the dismissal of legal proceedings, financial compensation for the defendant or the awarding of punitive damages, the court had to first of all determine, on a balance of probabilities, the absence of a reasonable expectation on the part of the party that had introduced the procedure or action that it could produce results that would be favourable to it at trial (section 5(1)), certainly a difficult task at the beginning of proceedings. It then had to determine that the proceeding or claim introduced had the primary purpose of dissuading the defendant or other actors from engaging in public participation, of diverting their resources to the legal proceedings or else of penalizing them for engaging in public participation (section 1(2)). To be considered illegitimate, a proceeding or claim had to meet these two cumulative criteria.

Since these requirements were demanding, the legislation proposed a kind of compensatory mechanism *a posteriori* to permit the defendant who had failed to convince the court to dismiss the proceeding or claim against him or her. If the defendant was able to demonstrate that there was a "realistic possibility" that the proceedings against him or her concealed illegitimate intentions as a result of public participation, the defendant could obtain an order that the plaintiff provide the court with a "security" to cover both the legal costs incurred and the punitive damages that would be awarded if the legal action was eventually ruled illegitimate (section 5(4)(a)).[49] The court also reserved the right to approve any settlement or abandonment of proceedings as well as the terms related to termination. This was in order to ensure that the party that had introduced a proceeding or claim for improper purposes did not get off scot-free by quickly abandoning the proceedings after an unanticipated setback or the submission of its adversary.

The provincial election in the spring of 2001 sounded the death knell for the British Columbia anti-SLAPP law. It would be quickly repealed by the new government. This repeal, according to the new legislative authorities, was to avoid having the law become an additional burden on the legal apparatus. No anti-SLAPP bill has been introduced in British Columbia since.

A First Anti-SLAPP Bill: The New Brunswick Model

Although British Columbia was the first Canadian province to adopt an anti-SLAPP law, it was preceded, in the legislative work on the issue, by New Brunswick, the first Canadian province to attempt to curtail strategic lawsuits against public participation in its jurisdiction.

The Legislative Assembly of New Brunswick received a first bill to fight legal intimidation of politically and socially active citizens in 1997. New Brunswick was then dealing with a number of lawsuits publicly considered to be SLAPPs, which prompted political actors with a certain proximity to civil society associations to call for legislation on the issue.

The New Brunswick bill, entitled *Public Participation Act* (Bill 102), included a number of interesting features that distinguished it from other later initiatives in the common law provinces (see Weir 2004). It included a lengthy preamble defining the social and political objectives of the proposed legislation. This preamble specified, for example, that it was incumbent on the legislator to act:

> Whereas the right of citizens to participate freely in the process of the government is fundamental to the functioning of our democratic system;
>
> Whereas this right is seriously undermined by civil actions brought primarily to chill citizen participation or otherwise to harass or intimidate citizens and citizens' organizations;
>
> And whereas there is need to reform the legal system to discourage the bringing of such actions.

SLAPPs are primarily defined as infringements on the right of New Brunswick citizens to participate in the process of government. This approach therefore resembles that favoured in the United States. The bill formally defined the "right of participation" presented as follows:

> Every person has a right to participate fully in the process of government including the right to petition and communicate with the government, and enjoys the freedom of expression, association and demonstration on matters of public policy. (section 3)

All the provisions in the bill revolved around this right of participation.[50] The bill specified in particular that any person who considered that a legal action against him or her infringed on this right could present a motion to have it dismissed. This motion would be studied according to an accelerated procedure (made up of, among other things, arguments and evidence by affidavit) and granted to the defendant if the plaintiff was not capable of establishing "on a clear and compelling basis that":

a) the action [brought against the defendant] is not one to which the Act applies;
b) in the alternative, that:
   i) the acts of the applicant lacked any reasonable basis in fact;
   ii) the applicant's primary purpose was to harass the respondent, or pursue some other private purpose other than the free exercise of the rights protected by this Act, and;
   iii) the acts of the applicant were the direct cause of a real injury to the respondent. (section 7)

This process was thus intended to reverse the burden of proof: the defendant, normally placed in a defensive position of justifying his or her actions, is freed from this to the detriment of a plaintiff that now has to justify the proceedings brought against its adversary (section 7). The defendant whose motion for dismissal was accepted would be automatically granted reimbursement of his or her expenses and legal fees. He or she could be granted punitive damages, if the court so ruled. The defendant making a motion for dismissal was authorized to accompany it with a claim for damages against the party that had brought the legal action. These damages would be *automatically* granted[51] if the motion was granted and the Court was satisfied that the Plaintiff filed the action for the purpose of:

a) harassment [of the defendant];
b) inhibiting the person's exercise of protected rights under this Act, or;
c) otherwise injuring the person. (section 9)

These provisions — quick dismissal of the abusive lawsuit, reversal of the burden of proof, financial compensation and awarding of damages — would have contributed to the protection of the right of participation defined by the bill. This bill, however, did not go beyond first reading in the Legislative Assembly of New Brunswick and was eventually dropped from the order paper of the province.

The Nova Scotia and Ontario Revivals of the British Columbia Model and a Cause for Legislative Hope in Ontario

Nova Scotia considered adopting a private member's anti-SLAPP bill, introduced in 2001 and reintroduced in 2003. Presented for first reading, the bill was never passed by the Nova Scotia Legislature. Entitled the *Protection of Public Participation Act*, this bill was intended to formally encourage public participation, dissuade the use of the legal system for improper purposes and preserve access to justice. The Nova Scotia bill appeared to copy the model proposed in British Columbia two years earlier and borrowed its main provisions.

Similarly, legislative action against SLAPPs in Ontario has taken inspiration from the British Columbia model. Although its fate is still uncertain, the Ontario initiative is, so far, the most promising. In recent years, certain cases publicly called SLAPPs by various commentators have highlighted a trend toward the abusive political instrumentalization of courts in the province (see, for example, Gray 2007; Smith 2008). The Ontario Legislative Assembly thus debated Bill 138 in December 2008. This bill, which had the title *An Act to encourage participation in public debate, and to dissuade persons from bringing legal proceedings or claims for an improper purpose,* was intended as a copy of the initiative proposed in British Columbia seven years earlier.[52] The Ontario version had the following objectives:

> The Bill protects persons from being subjected to legal proceedings that would stifle their ability to speak out on public issues or to promote, in the public interest, action by the public or by any level of government. Provision is made in the Bill for such legal proceedings to be dismissed at an early stage, for defendants subjected to such proceedings to be indemnified for the costs they incur in responding to those proceedings and for the court or tribunal to award additional damages to those defendants in appropriate circumstances. Communication or conduct constituting public participation is expressly designated as an occasion of qualified privilege in relation to all persons who become aware of that communication or conduct.

The provincial election in autumn 2011, however, meant that the legislative initiative died on the order paper. However, the process has been resumed since. Anti-SLAPP bills were submitted to the Ontario Legislative Assembly in 2012 and 2013.

The fate of the New Brunswick and Nova Scotia bills was largely the result of political circumstances: they were introduced by minority opposition groups and were consequently not given priority by the authorities in power. A similar fate very certainly awaited the first Ontario anti-SLAPP legislative initiative, which was brought forward by a member of the opposition.[53] Various Ontario groups therefore lobbied the government to make the anti-SLAPP struggle a priority.[54] The Ontario government acknowledged these groups and mandated an advisory panel to study potential legislative changes that could favour the prompt dismissal of abusive lawsuits and penalize their instigators.[55] This panel submitted its final recommendations to the Ontario government in October 2010 (see Moran et al. 2010).

Although they contained certain inconsistencies and omissions, the recommendations formulated by the advisory panel could lead, if accepted, to the adoption of an anti-SLAPP legislative model that could become an international model in countries with a common law legal tradition. On the one hand, and this is essential, the committee calls for the adoption of an anti-SLAPP law and considers it essential to protect the fundamental political role played by discussion and public participation:

> Participation by members of the community in matters of public interest is fundamental for democratic society. The very fabric of democracy is woven daily from the acts of citizens who engage in public discussion and contribute in countless ways to creating a civil society alive to the interests and rights of its members. It will always be important to recognize and protect these activities, but more than ever it seems crucial to encourage public participation as voter turnouts decline, society's needs become ever more complex and individuals feel increasingly powerless to effect meaningful change. If anything, public activities by individuals and groups within the community are even more essential in the face of such realities, and yet undertaking them has never been more challenging. (para. 4)

Moreover, the recommendations formulated by the report move away, appropriately, from the question of the *intentions* behind the lawsuits that have the *effect* of gagging social and political opposition. While it is proper to punish the instigators of lawsuits for improper purposes — in this case intimidation and legal repression of citizen participation in public debates — it is important first of all, according to the authors of the report, to protect citizens from lawsuits judicializing their public activities. It is therefore important to move away from the legislative models of British Columbia (and therefore, the failed legislative initiative in Nova Scotia) and New Brunswick, which were based on determination of the intentions of the plaintiff.[56] So what mechanism is proposed by the experts in order to protect the public participation of Ontario citizens?

The bill proposed that an expedited process, in which a motion to dismiss the action because of unwarranted interference with the public participation of the defendant, would be heard within sixty days of the motion to the court being filed; then, the suspension of the usual interlocutory proceedings until the motion to dismiss was considered; and above all, this process would no longer be based on the subjective determination of the plaintiff's motives and intentions, but on an analysis of the factual elements of the case. This would be done in three stages.

The court would first of all determine if the lawsuit involves a communication on a matter of public interest. The defendant would have the burden of proving this to the court on the balance of probabilities.

Once this request had been met, the onus would shift to the plaintiff to show that:

1) On the factual record, that the plaintiff's claim has substantial merit, and;
2) There are substantial grounds to believe that the defendant has no valid defence.

Finally, if the plaintiff meets these tests, it would still have to show the court that it has been caused *significant harm* by its adversary. Minor harm, even demonstrated, could not be used as a pretext for a legal dispute that could have disproportionate impact on freedom of expression on a matter of public interest. In other words, minor legal infractions committed by the defendant during public controversies — frequent, for example, in many cases of civil disobedience — should not provide a legal foundation permitting the plaintiff to break the backs of its adversaries in the courts. Failure to demonstrate the severity of the harm suffered would lead to dismissal of the legal action and reimbursement of costs incurred by the defendant. The court could also, if it determined that the proceedings that had been brought before it were intended to punish, silence or intimidate the defendant, award damages to the plaintiff (para. 46).

This mechanism is augmented by a number of provisions. First, the committee calls for qualified privilege for persons with a direct stake in a matter of public interest that they are commenting on or discussing publicly (para. 75). The communications carried out in good faith by these people would thus be protected. In addition, the committee recommends the suspension of public proceedings on issues associated with the actions and communications of the defendant (for which the defendant is being sued) until the motion to dismiss has been ruled on. This is done in order to avoid the legal proceedings reducing the capacity of the various parties to be heard by the public proceedings (para. 47).

The mechanism proposed by the Ontario advisory panel to curb SLAPPs is thus highly effective. It avoids the pitfalls associated with the determination of the plaintiff's intentions — which, unfortunately, is too often a key part of anti-SLAPP mechanisms — and proposes both an expedited process and the reimbursement of the costs incurred by the parties who have participated in good faith in public debate. This being said, the proposal is not without weaknesses.

First of all, the experts tend to confuse, like many commentators, gag suits and strategic lawsuits against public participation. The stated objective of the legislative reform presented in this report is to permit the quick identification and appropriate management of SLAPPs. However, that is not what is actually being proposed. A SLAPP is a deliberate, planned and organized strategy of legal intimidation (see Chapter 1). The reforms proposed in this report do not seek primarily to counteract intentional attempts at legal muzzling, but rather to prevent debates of public interest from becoming judicialized. This is not the same thing. Dropping the criterion of intentionality, associated with SLAPPs by the authors of the report, is not aimed therefore at circumventing legal obstacles to the quick identification and dismissal of SLAPPs, but to extend the protection offered from lawsuits that interfere unduly with public debate, whether or not this interference is collateral damage to the lawsuit or its primary objective. It is only incidentally that this report proposes penalizing those who have *deliberately* used the legal system to muzzle social and political opposition.[57] This logic is indisputably the best suited to protect citizen participation in public debate; nevertheless, clarification of the concepts is required.

The authors of the report refrain from recommending that parties that feel they have been sued following public participation be provided funding by a specific mechanism, maintaining that the provision of a quick hearing of the motion to dismiss as well as *a posteriori* compensation resulting from dismissal of the lawsuit are effective measures. They also refuse to propose the implementation of punitive measures for lawyers who have agreed to bring improper proceedings to the courts, claiming that they are already held responsible for their actions. This reasoning is tautological: obviously, the proliferation of lawsuits that appear to be SLAPPs in Ontario proves that the current rules do not have a sufficient dissuasive effect on legal experts who take on problematic cases. As such, measures need to be adopted in this area.

Finally, the authors avoid supporting the boldest recommendations that were proposed to them, in particular with respect to the removal of the right of corporations to sue for defamation, an overhaul of the tax system to eliminate tax deductions by companies for the costs associated with legal disputes (deductions that are not available to individuals) and the removal of the right of politicians to sue for defamation. Introduced in 2013 by the Liberal minority government, Bill 83, entitled the *Protection of Public Participation Act, 2013*, takes up many of the proposals formulated by the panel report.[58] As I write these lines, the bill had received second reading.

A Few Points of Analysis

The study of American, Australian and Canadian anti-SLAPP legislative initiatives illustrates a number of fundamental issues on this subject. The laws discussed differ first of all in their basic objectives. Some seek essentially to ensure the protection of citizen participation, which is considered crucial in democracy (seen, in the United States, from the perspective of the right to petition and, in Canada and Australia, from the perspective of the right of public participation), from the judicialization of social and political controversies. It is not a matter so much here of preventing and repressing lawsuits with malicious intentions as discouraging the judicialization of private conflicts arising from political differences expressed in the public arena. Such provisions are still controversial and are related to the question of the personal responsibility of individuals taking part in public debate. They primarily target and fight gag suits and only incidentally address SLAPPs.

Other legislative initiatives emphasize respect for individual rights — and in particular the right to reputation, which is frequently violated during public controversies — targeting more specifically the legal proceedings that hide improper intentions of repression and legal intimidation. The main objective of these legislative models is to prevent and repress SLAPPs. They are not very concerned about the observed trend among political adversaries to judicialize and privatize conflicts.

Regardless of the objectives of these laws, they can be effective in their respective mandates only if they satisfy a number of criteria. They should primarily — and this is imperative — permit the quick dismissal of the legal proceedings that they proscribe. This is not a foregone conclusion. Some laws rely on the common sense and judgment of the judiciary to achieve this; others prefer to restrict the judiciary by imposing precise, restrictive time limits. The American and Quebec experiences show that the adoption of anti-SLAPP legislation does not necessarily settle satisfactorily the question of legal entanglements for citizens who have participated in public debate. The unwieldiness of the legal apparatus and the prevailing legal culture are powerful obstacles to the prompt settlement of the disputes targeted by these laws.

Such provisions have to favour the quick reversal of the burden of proof: they need to lighten the task of defendants, relieve them of the legal and financial burden associated with preparing their defence and require the party that instigated legal proceedings interfering with the defendants' fundamental political rights to justify its legal action. This reversal of the burden of proof should oblige the plaintiff either to provide summary evidence on the foundations of the claim that they bring to the court (in order to avoid the prolongation of cases without legal foundation) or to provide additional evidence of the malicious nature of the communications or conduct directed against it by the defendant. The aim of this second option, in fact, is to immunize the infractions committed in good faith by citizens exercising their right to petition or their freedom of expression.

Most of the American and Canadian laws consider (quite rightly in my view) that the financial protection of SLAPP victims assumes a quick dismissal of the proceedings instigated against them. Most, however, fail to provide substantial protection that applies *during* legal proceedings — a failing that is all the more important given that many anti-SLAPP laws fail to provide rapid interruption of the proceedings to which they apply. The financial burden associated with the preparation of a defence, if only for the dismissal of an action, can be prohibitive for broad segments of the population. In spite of its weaknesses, the Quebec anti-SLAPP legislation presented in the next chapter includes in this respect an innovative mechanism that should, if it is applied properly by the courts, remedy this defect.

As the only Canadian province operating under a *civil law* legal system, Quebec has undertaken in recent years legislative measures to counteract strategic lawsuits against public participation. The Quebec case will be the specific subject of investigation in the next chapter.

Notes

1. There are also indications that SLAPPs exist in certain European countries with a civil law tradition. I do not, however, have the information necessary for the analysis of these cases and therefore will confine myself to a limited number of countries that share a common law legal tradition.

2. Other legal standards, in particular freedom of expression and public participation, are also applied, although to a lesser extent than the right to petition. See, for example, Stein 1989; McCarthy 1998.
3. This amendment reads as follows: "Congress shall make no law respecting an establishment of religion, or prohibiting the free exercise thereof; or abridging the freedom of speech, or of the press; or the right of the people peaceably to assemble, and to petition the Government for a redress of grievances (without fear of punishment or reprisal)."
4. This being said, American legislation currently tends to move away from an approach focusing exclusively on the right to petition and to introduce broader concepts of public participation and freedom of expression.
5. For an analysis of the constitutional jurisprudence on the right to petition, see Pring and Canan 1996.
6. This law defines public participation as follows: "'Public participation' means speech or lawful conduct that is genuinely aimed in whole or in part at procuring favorable government action" (section 554.01. sub.6.). This is a restrictive interpretation of the concept of public participation that is in line with the usual definitions of an act of petition. Other broader approaches include actions to influence public opinion that have little to do with communications aimed at obtaining favourable outcomes from public authorities.
7. "Lawful conduct or speech that is genuinely aimed in whole or in part at procuring favorable government action is immune from liability, unless the conduct or speech constitutes a tort or a violation of a person's constitutional rights" (section 554.03).
8. The boundaries of freedom of expression, public participation and right to reputation are frequently defined mutually: some anti-SLAPP laws have the primary objective of rebalancing these rights in a way that avoids having concepts of freedom of expression and public participation subordinated to the right to reputation, for example.
9. See Chapter 1 on this topic.
10. Since the protections offered by section 425.16 have themselves been abused by various actors in order to, for example, obtain an advantage over competitors, California legislators adopted section 425.17 to penalize its misuse.
11. Of course, this legislation is part of a specific legal culture and cannot be fully exported abroad, since some of the provisions that they contain could be incompatible with the economy of law prevalent in other jurisdictions. The California law, however, does contain some interesting principles and mechanisms.
12. Note here an extension of the protection offered to freedom of expression; this expresses a willingness to protect not only healthy communication between representatives and the represented, but also the smooth functioning of public debates.
13. The considerable importance given to the right to reputation in Quebec law reduces the appeal of a procedure of reversal of the burden of proof; it would be easy for the plaintiff to demonstrate that the legal procedure undertaken could lead to a favourable result.
14. "*A cause of action against a person arising from any act of that person in furtherance of the person's right of petition or free speech under the United States or California Constitution in connection with a public issue shall be subject to a special motion to strike, unless the court determines that the plaintiff has established that there is a probability that the plaintiff will prevail on the claim*" (section 425.16. (b) (1)).
15. The lawyers for the party that instigated the SLAPP are also subject to countersuits.

16. For an overview of these processes and the current progress of the legislation, see *The Public Participation Project* at <www.anti-slapp.org>.
17. The party instigating legal action against an adversary who had exercised his or her right to petition would have to demonstrate that this adversary had made allegations knowing they were false or with reckless disregard of evidence of falsity (section 3).
18. This removal would not be mandatory: the respondent could also take advantage of the anti-SLAPP provisions existing in the jurisdiction (if such measures exist).
19. The party that wants to take advantage of this provision would have to demonstrate *prima facie* before the court that the legal action instituted arises from an immunized activity or the exercise of a constitutional right to petition or freedom of expression. Once this requirement is met, the burden is shifted to the plaintiff, which would have to demonstrate *prima facie* both the legal foundation of the case and present the facts that are likely to give them a favourable verdict. Failure of the plaintiff to satisfied these demands will lead to the dismissal or cancellation of the case or the discovery proceedings identifying people or groups who have exercised their constitutional rights (section 7 (b)).
20. A detailed presentation of the case, as well as the text of the application instituting proceedings, can be found at <www.gunns20.org>.
21. The document quoted, entitled *Public Interest Lawyers' Statement in Support of Public Participation Law Reform*, is dated April 10, 2006, and is available online at <www.wilderness.org.au/files/fr_Lawyers_Statement re_PP.pdf>.
22. Nevertheless, successive decisions by the High Court of Australia have implicitly defined the parameters of such rights. The political and legal life of the country has been marked by recurrent debates on the relevance and need for the adoption of a legislative document specifying and detailing the rights and freedoms of Australian citizens. In addition, there have been various legislative initiatives in the Australian states to define the rights and freedoms of their residents. See, for example, the *Human Rights Act*, adopted by the Australian Capital Territory in 2004: <www.legislation.act.gov.au/aZ2004-5/current/pdf/2004-5.pdf>.
23. The proposed reform was supposed to be adopted by the different Australian states and territories. This quotation is from the law adopted by Queensland on November 18, 2005. See Queensland, *Defamation Act 2005,* 2006: <http://www.legislation.qld.gov.au/LEGISLTN/ CURRENT/D/DefamA05.pdf>.
24. This point was raised by Green M.P. Lee Rhiannon during a parliamentary debate on the reform of the Australian defamation law. In particular, she declared: "While powerful individuals can use defamation law to silence criticisms, corporations in recent times have turned to other areas of the law to commit what commentators have termed 'legal blackmail.' Tort litigation in the form of SLAPP suits has been used by corporations in Australia since the 1990s. It is one of those very unfortunate aspects of American life that has been imported into this country. SLAPP suits are brought by corporations or sometimes by wealthy individuals to silence critics." Parliament of New South Wales, debates of October 19, 2005. The transcripts of the parliamentary debates are online on the site of the Parliament of New South Wales, <www.parliament.nsw.gov.au>.
25. The Tasmanian bill preceded the national reform on defamation that took place in Australia.
26. This point is important; it would become impossible for a plaintiff to claim compensation for nonfinancial damages (damage to reputation or honour, psychological distress

such as anxiety, etc.), with financial compensation considered only, in the area of defamation, if the plaintiff can demonstrate that it has suffered quantifiable financial loss resulting from the action, conduct or communication of the respondent.
27. Tasmania, *Protection of Public Participation Bill 2005*, 2005. The text of the bill is online on the site of the Parliament of Tasmania: <www.parliament.tas.gov.au>.
28. Only technical details related to the Tasmanian legal system differed from the legislation adopted in British Columbia.
29. The legislative stages associated with the bill are presented on the site of the Parliament of Tasmania: <www.parliament.tas.gov.au/bills/Bills2005/14_of_2005.htm>.
30. See the bills entitled *Protection of Public Participation Bill 2005, 2006* and *2008*, online on the site of the government of South Australia: <www.legislation.sa.gov.au/listAZ-Bills.aspx?key=P>.
31. The standardization of the legislative framework with regard to defamation taking place in Australia could have been a factor on this point.
32. The bill defines the concept of public participation as follows: *"public participation means communication or conduct aimed (in whole or in part) at influencing public opinion, or promoting or furthering action by the public, a corporation or government body in relation to an issue of public interest."* It excludes, however, from the concept of "public participation" discriminatory communications aimed at certain groups, threatening to cause physical injury or damage to property, or constituting trespass on private property (sections 5 (1) and 5 (2)).
33. The text of the law is online on the site of the government of the Australian Capital Territory: <www.legislation.act.gov.au/a/2008-48/20080912-37699/pdf/2008-48.pdf>.
34. It is, however, likely that such lawsuits occurred earlier. However, only with the publicizing of the phenomenon identified by Pring and Canan in the early 1990s in the United States and in Canada would this practice be highlighted and SLAPP cases identified as such.
35. See *Daishowa Inc. v. Friends of the Lubicon, Kevin Thomas, Ed Bianchi, Stephen Kenda, Jane Doe, John Doe, and Persons Unknown*, O.J. No 1429 (Ont. S.C.J.), 1998: <www.lubicon.ca/pa/forestp/daifolp/decision.htm>.
36. This small amount had been requested by the plaintiff itself, which recognized that the respondent would not have the financial means to pay a more substantial sum. See *Daishowa Inc. v. Friends of the Lubicon, Kevin Thomas, Ed Bianchi, Stephen Kenda, Jane Doe, John Doe, and Persons Unknown*, 1998.
37. The court declared: "My conclusion is that if the Canadian Constitution protects a corporation's expression where the context is largely economic, and where one of the consequences of the expression, if accepted by the listener, might well be economic harm to competitors, then the common law should not erect barriers to expression by consumers where the purpose and effect of the expression is to persuade the listener to use his or her economic power to challenge a corporation's position on an important economic and public policy issue. The plight of the Lubicon Cree is such an issue, as is Daishowa's connection to it." (*Daishowa Inc. v. Friends of the Lubicon, Kevin Thomas, Ed Bianchi, Stephen Kenda, Jane Doe, John Doe, and Persons Unknown*, 1998: para. 82)
38. See "As of May 4, 2000, the Daishowa v. Friends of the Lubicon court battle has ended signaling closure in a twelve year long dispute between Daishowa and the Lubicon Nation," May 4, 2000: <http://tao.ca/~fol/pa/forestp/daifolp/po000504.htm>.

39. The preparation of the defence of the members of the Friends of Lubicon targeted by the suit instituted by Daishowa was made more complex by their inability to assume the costs associated with providing solid legal expertise. The members of the organization had to make do with *pro bono* legal representation and the support of the Sierra Legal Defence Fund. See Tollefson 1996.
40. See *Fraser v. Saanich (District)*, B.C.J. No. 3100 (B.C. S.C.) (QL), 1999.
41. The Canadian *Charter of Rights and Freedoms* also does not give freedom of expression a predominance similar to that accorded to the right to petition by the first amendment of the United States Constitution. While the right to petition is at the pinnacle of the American constitutional structure, superseding a whole set of important rights in relationship to SLAPP cases (in particular the right to reputation), in Canada, freedom of expression and the other rights outlined in the Charter are intended to be balanced. The inevitable result of this balance is a tension between potentially contradictory rights.
42. This is supported by Sankoff (2004: 103): "The Charter was expressly designed as a tool to restrain government action against individuals and was not created with the intention of altering the conduct of non-government actors who are the primary participants in civil proceedings. As such, the Charter's impact will understandably be less significant in this arena."
43. It would seem, however, that the Canadian *Charter of Rights and Freedoms* could have some application in the cases opposing private parties but that have clear "public" dimensions. It would thus be possible to use the Charter in private conflicts that go beyond the rights of the parties concerned to be part of broader issues of public interest (see Tollefson 1996).
44. Unlike the Canadian *Charter of Rights and Freedoms*, the Quebec *Charter of Human Rights and Freedoms* does not only have the legal goal to protect persons residing in Quebec from abuses by the government but also to "harmonize the relationships of Québec's citizens among themselves and with their institutions, in a context respectful of human dignity." The Quebec Charter has the function of defining the general rules that apply to collective life in Quebec. It therefore applies not only to governments, but also to any individual, group or private corporation resident in Quebec, except for the institutions under federal jurisdiction. It follows from this that freedom of expression has more extensive application in Quebec than in the rest of the country since it can be used against legal persons (corporations) or physical persons (neighbours, employers), as well as the provincial government. This broader application partly explains repeated reference to the right to freedom of expression by anti-SLAPP activists in Quebec and the development of a legislative response to the phenomenon that is based on this concept.
45. This argument has, for example, been made by Lott (2004): "The lack of constitutional protection for those subject to a SLAPP suit in Canada also supports an argument for the need for specific legislative protections against SLAPPs. Because SLAPPs are usually private actions, not involving government actors, defendants of SLAPPs cannot invoke the free expression rights found in the Canadian *Charter of Rights and Freedoms*, because it does not apply to private actions."
46. The concept of the right to "public participation" is crucial in the anti-SLAPP legislative models considered in the Canadian common law provinces. In the absence of clear constitutional protection for freedom of expression that can be applied with

respect to SLAPPs, it was considered necessary to reframe the issues associated with this concept around the question of public participation. The main objective of the British Columbia legislation was, obviously, to protect public participation from attempts at judicial extortion by SLAPPers. The concept of "participation" excludes all illegal communication or conduct, any infraction of norms and standards in the area of human rights and of court orders, any action causing damage to the private property of others, and any unwarranted interference with the rights or property of another person (section 1(1)).

47. The anti-SLAPP legislative mechanisms presented here also apply for the Tasmanian bill presented previously.
48. The many similarities between the law adopted in British Colombia and the legislative models proposed subsequently in Australia suggest that the British Columbia legislation actually influenced the legislation in that country. Some authors have also noted this influence (see Bover and Parnell 2001).
49. The law also included provisions permitting the court to impose on a plaintiff that has abandoned its legal action in the course of the proceedings to reimburse the legal and extralegal costs incurred by the respondent. This provision was intended to ensure that SLAPPs were not abandoned in the course of the proceedings without penalty for their instigators.
50. This right of participation is extensive and excludes only "an action against a person for deliberate destruction of property or the deliberate infliction of physical injury to other persons" (section 10).
51. The bill is clear on this point: if the court grants the motion to dismiss from the defendant and is satisfied of the abusive nature of the intentions of the plaintiff, it "shall award the person actual damages and may award punitive damages" (section 9).
52. Except for a few minor modifications, the only appreciable addition in the Ontario bill to the legislative initiative adopted in British Columbia was in giving the court of justice or administrative tribunal the power to suspend "any public consultation or approval process that is conducted by a government body" when it is related to a suit that is the subject of a motion to dismiss and/or compensation. This suspension could thus be applied until the court rules on the legitimate or illegitimate nature of the lawsuit. It seems to me that this measure was aimed at preventing the party that had introduced the proceedings with improper purposes from being able to impose their will in public consultations through legal entanglements created for its political adversaries (para. 4(4)).
53. Bill 138 was introduced as a private member's bill by opposition New Democrat MPP Andrea Horwath on December 9, 2008.
54. The anti-SLAPP efforts in Ontario are in particular spearheaded by Ecojustice, the Environmental Law Association and Environmental Defence. More than sixty groups and organizations also sent a petition to the Premier of Ontario asking for the adoption of anti-SLAPP provisions.
55. The consultation process adopted in Ontario was a close imitation of that favoured in Quebec a few years earlier. There will be more details on this in the next chapter. The Ontario advisory panel was made up of Mayo Moran, dean of the University of Toronto Law School, Brian MacLeod Rogers, a lawyer specializing in the media, and Peter Downard, a partner with Fasken Martineau.
56. The legislative model adopted in British Columbia was based, as explained above,

on the determination of the "improper purposes" of the lawsuit; the bill considered in New Brunswick required the plaintiff to demonstrate in the court the merits of its intentions.
57. The authors thus recommend that eventual anti-SLAPP legislation avoid using this acronym, precisely because it implies a qualification of the intentions of the plaintiff, which should, according to them, be eliminated. Ironically, they apply this same acronym throughout their report to refer to proceedings that do not necessarily arise from improper intentions. They repeatedly confuse "LAPP" (lawsuit against public participation, which I would call a gag suit) and "SLAPP."
58. Bill 83, *Protection of Public Participation Act*, 2013. See <http://www.ontla.on.ca/web/bills/bills_detail.do?locale=en&BillID=2810&detailPage=bills_detail_the_bill>.

Chapter 4

Fighting SLAPPs
The Quebec Experience

Over more than three years, Quebec saw the emergence and growth of a campaign of popular mobilization on strategic lawsuits against public participation. This campaign led to the adoption, in June 2009, of what I believe to be the only anti-SLAPP legislation passed in a *civil law* jurisdiction.

How can one fight the legal repression of citizen participation in public debate? First, politically: it is crucial to expose this practice, which is destructive to freedom, and publicly denounce the individuals, groups and corporations that have used the courts to judicially stifle their adversaries. Next, legally: each case must be crafted by the organization of a solid, broadly supported defence (a difficult task in itself). And, above all, legislatively: legislators must be pressured to make legal reforms in order to eradicate this practice.

In Quebec, citizens calling for the adoption of an anti-SLAPP law were successful in showing both the existence of the phenomenon within their jurisdiction (using a few key cases that mobilized the attention of the public and lawmakers), the need to act and the existence of legislative solutions that could curb the phenomenon. The campaign in Quebec is neither unique nor exceptional: there have been similar experiences in Australia and the United States. The Quebec experience in the anti-SLAPP struggle does, however, have a lot to teach us and can serve as a model or inspiration for groups of citizens elsewhere who want to fight the legal muzzling of political speech.

Getting SLAPPs Recognized

The fight against strategic lawsuits against public participation is both restricted and favoured by the very nature of the phenomenon. On the one hand, the subject is complex, technical and tedious. It is, after all, a phenomenon coloured by the law and the legal apparatus that administers it: it is therefore prone to domination by the discourse of accredited experts. Anti-SLAPP activists are at risk of getting lost in the twists and turns of legal rhetoric and failing to keep favourable public opinion alive. Moreover, and this is fundamental, SLAPPs affect standards, values and principles that could galvanize this same public opinion, as long as there is an effective communication strategy. Freedom of expression, the right of participation in public debate, the right to be informed and the right to a fair and equitable trial are all concepts that can touch the hearts and souls of people. The main problem is to raise awareness of these concepts: how can the issues associated with these lawsuits be framed in order to reach the various publics that anti-SLAPP activists want to address? The answer to this question was spontaneous in Quebec.[1]

Citoyens, Taisez-Vous!

The organization of a Quebec anti-SLAPP campaign can largely be credited to social mobilization activities launched by two environmental organizations. In October 2006, the Association québécoise de lutte contre la pollution atmosphérique (AQLPA), the Comité de restauration de la Rivière Etchemin (CRRE) and a handful of activists launched the campaign *Citoyens, taisez-vous!*[2] This campaign, among other things, organized a solidarity movement around the AQLPA, the CRRE and citizens, who were sued for more than 5 million dollars by American Iron & Metal (AIM), a metal recycling company. The lawsuit was called a SLAPP from the beginning by various commentators from the social, legal and journalistic communities, who saw it has an outrageous attempt at the legal muzzling of citizen expression (see, for example, Breton 2006; Bourgault-Côté 2006; Margonty 2006).

Citoyens, taisez-vous! poster

Roméo Saganash, then of the Grand Council of the Crees (upper left), Yann Perreau, singer (upper right), André Bélisle, AQLPA (lower left) and Julius Grey, lawyer (lower right)

Citoyens, taisez-vous! was the beginning of social mobilization on the SLAPP in Quebec and alerted public opinion on the issue. This campaign also put pressure on lawmakers to adopt provisions to protect the citizens of Quebec from improper legal proceedings and to financially support the defence of groups and individuals targeted by these lawsuits. The AQLPA, which had led the campaign, set up a website devoted to its defence and public education on SLAPPs.[3] The association organized press conferences and media events, launched a petition to the National Assembly and developed a broad support network. More than fifty Quebec civil society groups officially gave their support to the campaign. The three big Quebec union federations, many public personalities as well as the main political parties of the province also expressed solidarity with the efforts of the organizers of *Citoyens, taisez-vous!*

The campaign would gradually peter out as a distinct movement between December 2007, the date of the out-of-court settlement between AIM and the defendants, and April 2008, when a broader Quebec anti-SLAPP coalition gradually crystallized and took the leadership with lobbying, grassroots education and media presence (I will come back to this).[4] Widely publicized, *Citoyens, taisez-vous!* used strong, evocative imagery to illustrate in simple terms what was, nevertheless, a complex legal and political phenomenon.

The red gag image quickly became the symbol of the anti-SLAPP movement and would be used many times during public events. Citizens and community groups would gag themselves publicly in specific, highly symbolic places — the National Assembly, the Superior Court, or during press conferences — in order to attract the attention of the media and generate public support for an eventual anti-SLAPP law. The campaign would have considerable effect. It served in particular to generate extensive media coverage and attract the attention of both the public and lawmakers in Quebec to certain cases that were troubling to say the least.[5] The imagery used by the anti-SLAPP activists expressed in strong terms the feelings of powerlessness, outrage and being muzzled experienced not only by the SLAPP victims, but also by those who, while not directly targeted by those lawsuits, were potential targets. This *"chilling effect"* that SLAPPs have on public mobilization was becoming apparent; family, friends and colleagues of the defendants, who did not want to be dragged before the courts in turn, tended to feel muzzled as much as their less fortunate associates.

With the launch of the *Citoyens, taisez-vous!* campaign, the activists demanded that Quebec legislators act and adopt a law to protect the citizens of Quebec against strategic lawsuits against public participation.[6] The provincial official opposition fully backed these demands and publicly asked the then Minister of Justice, Yvon Marcoux, to intervene to counteract practices of legal intimidation occurring in Quebec.[7]

An Expert Panel

The efforts of Quebec civil society groups quickly bore fruit. A few days before the official launch of the campaign in October 2006, the Minister of Justice mandated an expert panel to evaluate the situation in Quebec around the issue of SLAPPs. This panel was to:

> Make an assessment of the current rules in Quebec, Canada and the United States on the balance between freedom of expression and the right to reputation, and between the right to go to court and the reasonable nature of actions. If it appeared that Quebec law did not permit the maintenance of a fair balance, the panel would have a mandate to explore improvements that could be made to it. (MacDonald et al. 2007: 94)

Made up of Professor Pierre Noreau, Professor Daniel Jutras and chaired by Professor Roderick A. Macdonald, the expert panel submitted its report to the government in March 2007. Entitled *Les poursuites stratégiques contre la mobilisation publique — les poursuites-bâillons* (SLAPP) (or the Macdonald Report), this report was made public in July of the same year.

The report played a decisive political role in the organization of an anti-SLAPP campaign in Quebec. It was primarily an educational tool in accessible language that was used by many actors in Quebec civil society. The existing literature on strategic lawsuits against public participation remains, in fact, mostly in English and usually intended for an American public that has a solid knowledge of the law. By summarizing the conclusions of many important works on the subject, by translating key elements into French and by contextualizing the issues associated with SLAPPs in the legal system and Quebec society, the Macdonald Report offered a first grassroots education platform on the issue, providing a basis upon which the different groups were able to work.

The report also established a framework on the basis of which Quebec lawmakers considered the issue of SLAPPs. The conclusions of the report thus had significant influence on both the work of the civil society groups and that of Quebec lawmakers. The authors of the report observed that:

> The phenomenon of the use of gag suits is a real phenomenon, even though it is not systematically practised in Quebec. The situations recently brought to light by the media reveal, however, that SLAPPs are an observable reality, and that they are a real threat to the participation of citizens and groups in public debate. In this specific sense, they constitute both a threat for participatory democracy and a true danger of diversion from the goals of the justice system. For this reason, it seems necessary to intervene in order to discourage these practices. More specifically, it seems imperative to the members of the panel that any policy related to the control of these practices meet the following objectives:
>
> 1) protection of the right to freedom of expression and public opinion;
> 2) quick dismissal of gag suits during proceedings;
> 3) dissuasion of those who initiate SLAPPs;
> 4) maintenance of the integrity and goals of the legal system;
> 5) access to justice. (2007: 76)

The expert panel therefore recommended that the government act according to these recommended measures, which could be implemented in order to curb the phenomenon. Quebec politicians reacted favorably to the report's recommendations and began the process that would lead to the study of possible legislation. The National Assembly mandated the Committee on Institutions to look into the problem of SLAPPs in Quebec. This would be done through the organization of public hearings on the issue that took place from February to April 2008, then, following the submission of a draft bill in June, special consultations in October of the same year.[8]

Public Consultations

The public consultations held in 2008 were dominated by a citizen perspective on SLAPPs. The public interest expressed through the consultation process countered the positions defended by economic lobbies in Quebec, which were hostile to the adoption of an anti-SLAPP law, and by the Quebec Bar, which was sceptical about the usefulness of legislative action. This can be explained quantitatively: the community groups overwhelmed the legal experts and the representatives of the business community with representations favourable to legislative action. Despite the tendency for the complex, technical and precise nature of these legal questions to result in the domination of the discourse by legal experts, this is not what happened.

Moreover, the public consultations generated a framework within which different organizations were able to organize, publicize their positions and establish a broad coalition to ensure leadership in the area of political lobbying and grassroots education. Thus, in addition to providing direct, unsupervised access to political decision-makers (a basic element in any process of political lobbying designed to be at all effective[9]), these consultations provided an opportunity to mobilize public opinion and strengthen bonds among the groups involved. During the public hearings held in early 2008, the Quebec Civil Liberties Union, the Réseau Québécois des groupes écologistes (RQGE) [Quebec Network of Ecology Groups], the Association québécoise de lutte contre la pollution atmosphérique [Quebec Association to Fight Atmospheric Pollution] and, subsequently, Éditions Écosociété, took the initiative in the anti-SLAPP struggle in Quebec and formed a coalition of interested parties.[10]

> During the public hearings, they said:
>
> Where are the rights of citizens, in this case, when the whole community is silenced? We live in a society of law, so shouldn't it be fair and equitable for everyone? How is it that it allows and permits corporations to sue us for millions to stop us from denouncing things that are harmful for everyone? It is urgent to pass legislation and create an anti-SLAPP law that would protect the rights of citizens, as there is in the United States, from those who abuse the rights of people ... in order to counteract the arrogance and zeal of those corporations that reign supreme and to end the regime of terror used by these corporations to restrict criticism of their operations or projects. (Christine Landry, citizen targeted by a 1.25 million dollar lawsuit, February 20, 2008)

What we see in the area of SLAPPs is that people are forced to sign agreements because often they have been thrown off balance. Not because they think they're wrong; they know they're right, and at least they were right to participate and say what they had to say. But they have given in because it is costing them too much, because they are exhausted, because they have lost their wife and kids, and because nobody will talk to them ... finally, even physically, this is what we see at all levels, and not only financially, physically, there are real effects on those people. (Stéphane Bédard, Opposition MNA, March 20, 2008)

Analyzing the problem as an infringement on the exercise of fundamental rights seems to us to be the fairest way to deal with it, since it denotes above all the problem of guaranteeing access to justice for all. The SLAPPers count on the lack of material and financial means of citizens who have to defend themselves in the justice system and use this difference in power. (Michel Sawyer, Secrétariat intersyndical des services publics [Inter-union Secretariat of Public Services], February 26, 2008)

Since the imbalance between the parties is present at all stages in the process, the right to a fair trial without having the appropriate financial or legal resources is denied to the activists and citizens. In fact, the most glaring observations are related to the imbalance in financial resources, which constitutes a direct denial of the rights of activists, in particular their right of access to justice and to a fair and equitable trial. How can you pay a competent lawyer when you have insufficient resources? How then can we assert our rights when we don't have all the appropriate means? (Gaétan Cousineau, Commission des droits de la personne et des droits de la jeunesse [Human Rights and Youth Rights Commission], March 18, 2008)

What we are proposing to you today are measures to re-establish public trust in the legal system, measures to improve access to justice for the citizens of Quebec, and access to justice includes access to justice for defendants. (Dominique Neuman, Association québécoise de lutte contre la pollution atmosphérique, February 20, 2008)

Okay, when one fine morning just like that, a bailiff shows up with a pile of files, what I mean is, I leafed through them, the files, when I received them, well, the formal notice. That, I mean, for us, was incomprehensible; it was in language we couldn't understand at all. We asked each other: what's happening? Who do we call? What's going on? Basically we feel completely vulnerable in a situation like that. (Marie-Ève Baupré, Quebec Friends of the Earth, March 18, 2008)

These groups calling for the adoption of an anti-SLAPP law thus established a strategy that would remain in effect throughout the subsequent campaign, that is, direct dialogue with lawmakers and simultaneous pressure on them by soliciting public opinion using media events. The public hearings held from February to April 2008 permitted the affirmation of a broad social consensus on the need to take legislative action to counteract SLAPPs and led to the involvement of the Minister of Justice in drafting legislation on the issue.

The Écosociété Case and the Introduction of the First Anti-SLAPP Bill

It would be unjust and dishonest to be silent on the role played by the publisher of the original version of this book in the process of social mobilization and political lobbying that led to the adoption of a Quebec anti-SLAPP law. I cannot avoid it.

On April 10, 2008, Éditions Écosociété received a formal notice from the biggest gold mining corporation in the world, Barrick Gold, demanding that it not publish the forthcoming book *Noir Canada — Pillage, corruption et criminalité en Afrique*, written by Alain Deneault, William Sacher and Delphine Abadie. This formal notice was based on previous analysis of the summary of the book and its table of contents, which were available online. The corporation alleged that the forthcoming book contained defamatory allegations prejudicial to its reputation.[11]

The launch of the book, planned for April 11, 2008, was cancelled.[12] Two days later, and notwithstanding the risks associated with the action, Écosociété nevertheless began distributing the book in bookstores, refusing to comply with the demands of its detractors. The authors of the book and the publisher, from the beginning, referred to the legal proceedings against them as legal intimidation very much resembling a SLAPP.[13] On April 29, 2008, the gold mining corporation took legal action and claimed 6 million dollars jointly from Écosociété and the three authors of the book: 5 million dollars in compensatory damages and 1 million dollars in punitive damages.[14]

The legal action taken by Barrick against Écosociété and the authors of *Noir Canada* was eventually accompanied by a second suit, this time launched in Ontario by the Banro mining company, which claimed in turn 5 million dollars for defamatory libel. Since they did not possess the financial resources necessary for their defence, Éditions Écosociété and the authors of *Noir Canada* were threatened with bankruptcy. They therefore began a public campaign for support and funding, launched a website presenting their case and denounced the lawsuits launched against them as SLAPPs aimed at muzzling public debate.[15]

The Quebec anti-SLAPP campaign was therefore given a second wind with this major legal case. The *Noir Canada* affair would remobilize social forces in the province on the issue of SLAPPs following the out-of-court settlement between the AQLPA and the plaintiff a few months earlier.

The obscene nature of the parameters of the lawsuits against Écosociété and the authors of *Noir Canada* perhaps explains the deep feelings of outrage that they generated in the Quebec population. The Barrick Gold mining corporation reported profits of 837 million U.S. dollars in the final quarter of 2010.[16] It was opposing before the courts a non-profit organization with annual revenues of $225,000 Canadian. The cumulative amounts of the two lawsuits against the publisher and the authors of *Noir Canada* would have thus been roughly equivalent to fifty years of annual income of the publishing house. All this for a title that, if it had not been for the publicity generated by the lawsuits, would probably only have sold a few hundred copies in Quebec. The image created certainly has not been to the advantage of the plaintiffs. Nearly five hundred Canadian intellectuals publicly expressed their support for Écosociété and the authors of *Noir Canada* and called the legal proceedings against them SLAPPs. Dozens of organizations did likewise.[17]

At the same time as these new developments were taking place, the Quebec Civil Liberties Union and the AQLPA organized in May 2008 a first e-mail campaign to the Minister of Justice, calling for the adoption of an anti-SLAPP law that included:

1) Recognition of the right to public participation;
2) The establishment of an emergency procedure to permit the quick dismissal of SLAPPs;
3) The reversal of the burden of proof in cases that appear to be SLAPPs;
4) Financial protection for SLAPP victims and penalties for their instigators; and
5) The possibility of cancelling the gag clauses in out-of-court settlements.

More than a thousand letters from some 150 groups and more than a thousand individuals would be sent to the Minister.[18]

Écosociété became a key player in the Quebec anti-SLAPP coalition, starting in June 2008 to take part in planning and organizing meetings and carrying out joint actions with other Quebec civil society groups on the SLAPP issue.[19] In response to these concerns, the Minister of Justice, Jacques Dupuis, introduced the first bill to counteract abusive lawsuits in Quebec on June 13, 2008.[20] The adjournment of the National Assembly for the summer, however, postponed adoption of the anti-SLAPP bill until autumn 2008.[21]

Special consultations took place in October 2008 on the anti-SLAPP bill (Bill 99). About twenty groups took part. To no one's surprise, these consultations became a forum for a revolt by representatives from the business community. They were the only ones to show open hostility to the bill during the special consultations.[22] Wondering "sincerely why the minister considered it a good idea to legislate on this matter at this time," the Conseil du patronat asked the Committee on Institutions "for what demonstrable reasons would we be the only jurisdiction in Canada to have anti-SLAPP provisions?" (Conseil du patronat du Québec 2008,

p. 6 for this passage, p. 7 and 11 for the following ones). The organization took the view that the provisions proposed by the bill were "completely disproportionate to a problem whose existence, with respect to gag suits at the very least, remains to be demonstrated." Consequently, the Conseil du patronat said that it did not believe in "the relevance of the bill as it had been drafted."

The Quebec federation of chambers of commerce also took the view that the bill would favour a "culture of controversy" and "paralyze even more major development projects in Quebec." According to the Federation, "this systematic opposition is very harmful to the reputation of all Quebec and could be a disadvantage in terms of attracting foreign investments." (Fédération des chambres de

> During the special consultations, they said:
>
> This context of gag suits is a manifestation of a [legal] system that is not working. (Jack R. Miller, citizen, October 15, 2008)
>
> The observation is often made in public debates that the turnout in elections is in sharp decline, and that means that our democracy is not healthy. But, in another way, you see that, more and more, people are doing politics or making interventions in the public sphere through other mechanisms, through various commissions, in NGOs, etc.... the sites and methods of public participation in major public debates are changing. People's involvement in politics is no longer only through electoral voting. This law asks us to imagine the possibility of public participation taking place through interventions in the public sphere, and therefore the extent of freedom of expression in our society for the future, in particular in the area of political questions, should be expanded and protected more than before. This bill envisages precisely this, and it is for this reason that we believe that Quebec was right to go forward, anticipate the way in which we can encourage political participation. (Roderick A. M. Macdonald, chair of the expert panel on SLAPPs, October 22, 2008)
>
> I think that people have to take responsibility for their actions. If I take a position, if I decide to step over a line with what I say and if those words are libellous, I have to take responsibility for it. (Gérald R. Tremblay, Quebec Bar, October 15, 2008)
>
> And it is not because there are few judgments handed down that this is not a widespread phenomenon. And I can tell you that it more often takes the form of indirect threats or I can tell you at most, often it comes in a formal notice or a letter applying pressure and, extremely rarely, of a lawsuit that is filed and that ends in a verdict. (Michel Bélanger, Centre québécois du droit de l'environnement, October 15, 2008)

commerce du Québec 2008: 5) The Federation declared that it did not believe that citizens "needed new legislation to express their points of view in public debates," the "frequent citizen opposition to economic development projects in recent years" being "proof" of this (5).

The opposition of the representatives of the business community, as well as the doubts previously expressed by the emissaries of the Quebec Bar with regard to the relevance and desirability of an anti-SLAPP law, were nevertheless marginalized in the discussions that took place between parliamentary representatives and Quebec civil society groups. This marginalization was reinforced by the unanimous desire shown by all the political parties with members in the National Assembly to take legislative action on the issue. This unanimity had already been achieved by the beginning of public hearings in February 2008.

Once political cohesiveness was achieved, the debates in the parliamentary commission dealt mainly with the ways in which the lawmakers of Quebec should act. On this point, opinions were the most divided. The discussions around what the legislative response to the SLAPP problem should be in Quebec were largely framed by the proposals in the Macdonald Report (MacDonald et al. 2007: 76–82). Three options were therefore proposed to the Quebec legislators: the drafting of a legislative text on SLAPPs that would establish new rights and duties between litigants; changes to the Code of Civil Procedure that would give the courts greater latitude to quickly quash improper legal proceedings and discourage the abusive use of the courts; and, finally, the adoption of an explicitly anti-SLAPP law that, while modifying the Code of Civil Procedure, would also explain in a preamble the objectives of the legislative action. In general, both for the lawmakers and for the actors favourable to the adoption of an anti-SLAPP law, the essential question was to determine which of the three options proposed by the report would be used as the main driver of an eventual legislative model. Different variants were studied on the basis of these options. A few initiatives, more radical in Quebec law, were not adopted. The Confédération des syndicats nationaux, for example, proposed that judicial immunity be granted to public organizations, ATTAC-Québec proposed the removal of the right of companies to sue for defamatory libel, and the Association québécoise de lutte contre la pollution atmosphérique called for the cancelation of gag clauses in out-of-court settlements.[23]

At the same time as this work was progressing, the members of the anti-SLAPP coalition undertook a joint evaluation of Bill 99 and organized a second letter-writing campaign calling for the adoption of an improved bill before the end of the parliamentary session. Nearly a thousand e-mails were sent to the members of the Committee on Institutions as well as to its chair, Lise Thériault. The Minister of Justice, Jacques Dupuis, also took advantage of the completion of the work of the Commission to announce his intention to legislate on the issue before the end of the parliamentary session.

The public announcement of a provincial general election, however, threatened the entire consultative and legislative process. The members of the anti-SLAPP coalition appealed to the Minister of Justice and all the members to adopt an improved bill before the provincial election was called, predicted for November 5, 2008. This appeal was to no avail: the election was called before the adoption of Bill 99, which died on the order paper. The political situation with respect to Bill 99 was therefore, for a time, rather paradoxical, since the election call had killed a legislative initiative that had the unanimous support of the National Assembly, that was called for by the two main political parties that did not have seats in that legislature (Québec solidaire and the Quebec Green Party), and that enjoyed a consensus in Quebec civil society.

The members of the anti-SLAPP coalition therefore took action to convince lawmakers to revive Bill 99 — and to avoid having the election call become a pretext for, or lead to, the abandonment of the legislative initiative — and to initiate an exception process to ensure the quick resumption of parliamentary work on this topic. A third letter-writing campaign was thus started in December 2008.[24] This letter-writing campaign, backed by more than 600 individuals and civil society groups in Quebec, was addressed to Jacques Dupuis, then Minister of Justice, Claude l'Écuyer, then justice critic for the official opposition, and Daniel Turp, justice critic for the second opposition party.

The reorganization of political forces in Quebec following the December 8, 2008, election increased the complexity of the lobbying process, without, however, weakening the determination of the political parties to adopt the legislation.[25] The members of the anti-SLAPP coalition nevertheless had difficulty at first establishing contact with the new Minister of Justice, Kathleen Weil, and organized a second public demonstration in front the courthouse in Montreal. This demonstration was initially intended to denounce the Minister's silence. The event, planned for March 5, 2009, took another turn when the Minister's political attaché informed the members of the anti-SLAPP coalition that the Minister would re-introduce a new bill "during the coming weeks" (see Alexandre Shields 2009).

The demonstration on March 5, 2009, in front of the courthouse thus changed in tone and demanded that the Minister of Justice "make a public commitment that a law to counteract gag suits would be adopted by the end of the coming parliamentary session, in June 2009" (Ligue des droits et libertés 2009). Around a hundred people, supported by more than sixty Quebec civil society organizations, took part. Minister Weil made a public commitment the same day to re-introduce an anti-SLAPP bill in the Quebec National Assembly.

The Resurrection of the Anti-SLAPP Bill and the Adoption of Law 9

On April 7, 2009, the Quebec Minister of Justice, Kathleen Weil, presented to the National Assembly Bill 9, *An Act to amend the Code of Civil Procedure to prevent improper use of the courts and promote freedom of expression and citizen participation in public debate.* Bill 9 retained the main provisions of the previous Bill 99, which had died on the order paper, with some significant improvements. The changes made were the result of the consultative process carried out in October 2008 on the previous Bill 99. The new version of Bill 9 thus expressed the Minister's evaluation of the changes that needed to be made to Bill 99 so that it could more effectively achieve its objectives.

A detailed study of Bill 9 took place on May 26, 2009. This study was the final opportunity for the various political parties in Quebec to influence the precise wording of the bill. The members of the anti-SLAPP coalition also did intensive lobbying with opposition groups so that they would be the political spokespersons for their concerns about Bill 9. Bill 9 was finally adopted on June 3, 2009, by the National Assembly and received royal assent the next day, becoming law on June 4, 2009. Quebec thus became the only Canadian province to have an anti-SLAPP law. The activities of the anti-SLAPP coalition were suspended after adoption of Law 9, since the legislative objectives of the coalition had been achieved.[26] Sporadic activities and meetings, as well as a vigil on SLAPPs, were organized during the month following the adoption of the legislation, but remained essentially one-time activities.[27]

Epilogue: The Écosociété Affair

Sued in Quebec and Ontario, Écosociété and the authors of *Noir Canada* undertook two complementary processes: move the Ontario lawsuit to Quebec and mobilize the provisions of Law 9 to get the two lawsuits quashed. The attempt to move the lawsuit brought by the Banro Corporation proved unsuccessful, since it was rejected by the Supreme Court.

As they said they would,[28] the defendants tried to use the new Law 9 to secure the dismissal of the lawsuit brought by the Barrick Gold mining company. In its verdict of August 12, 2011, the Quebec Superior Court refused to grant this request, declaring that although there were indications of abuse of proceedings, they were insufficient to justify dismissal of the action.[29]

Judge Guylène Beaugé nonetheless specified that "Barrick seems to be trying to intimidate the authors" with a "procedural behaviour that appears immoderate," pointing out the "disproportionate" nature of the legal actions.[30] In spite of this observation, Barrick Gold has always denied having brought an improper lawsuit[31] and justified the proceedings against its adversaries, claiming that the allegations against it are false and attributable to "the negligence, recklessness, and ill will of the authors."[32] Noting the economic imbalances between the parties and the appearance of abuse, the Court awarded a provision for costs of $143,000 to the defendants.

Whether or not the lawsuit was abusive will never, it seems, be determined by a court verdict. Éditions Écosociété announced it had concluded an out-of-court agreement with Barrick Gold on October 18, 2011. In its news release, the publisher specified that it wanted to "free itself of a 40-day trial and the many proceedings representing in themselves colossal financial, human and moral costs" and announced that it was ceasing publication of the book *Noir Canada*.[33] On April 26, 2013, five years after the beginning of the proceedings, Éditions Écosociété announced it had also settled out-of-court with Banro. The publisher's spokesperson, Anne-Marie Voisard, presented this settlement as being the "best solution," while adding that "the legal process is so slow and onerous that it is likely to exhaust us financially before we can defend ourselves before the courts" (Shields 2013).

The out-of-court agreement between Éditions Écosociété and Barrick Gold elicited mixed reactions in the Quebec population. Some deplored a victory for censorship and the cancelation of the publication of the book (see Cloutier 2011); others called into doubt the effectiveness of the Quebec anti-SLAPP law, since it had proven incapable of facilitating the prompt dismissal of the proceedings targeting Écosociété and the three authors of *Noir Canada*. Some also pointed out the public relations disaster that this case became for the mining company (Dickner 2011).

I see things a little differently. Beyond the discussions on the merits of the lawsuit or whether it should have been called a gag suit or SLAPP, it should be underlined that the imbalance of the forces involved was such that it was highly unlikely that the independent publisher and the authors could have survived financially three years of legal proceedings. We would have expected the publisher to soon either go out of business or else make profuse public excuses (which it never did).[34] The economic imbalance, real and substantial, was recognized by the judiciary only three years after the beginning of the proceedings and two years following the adoption of the Quebec anti-SLAPP law.[35] The measures endorsed by the Superior Court to reduce the impacts — the awarding of a provision for costs — would remain palliative and incapable of mitigating the extent of the inequality of resources that could be invested by protagonists opposing each other in the legal arena. The Écosociété affair illustrates not so much the limitations of the Quebec anti-SLAPP law as a systemic failure of our justice system to ensure a legal process that is as equitable as possible and immune from economic influences.

Analysis of Law 9

The adoption of an anti-SLAPP law in Quebec was the end result of three years of efforts carried out by civil society groups, intellectuals concerned about the issue and MNAs who were sensitive to the protection of freedom of expression. Entitled *An Act to amend the Code of Civil Procedure to prevent improper use of the courts and promote freedom of expression and citizen participation in public debate*, Law 9 modified the Code of Civil Procedure through a framework law explaining the aims of the legislator. These intentions are spelled out in the explanatory notes attached to the legislation, which read as follows:

> This bill amends the Code of Civil Procedure to promote freedom of expression and prevent abusive use of the courts, in particular the use of

court proceedings to thwart the right of citizens to participate in public debate.

For that purpose, the bill allows the courts to promptly dismiss any abuse of procedure. It specifies what may constitute an abuse of procedure and authorizes the reversal of the burden of proof if the abuse of procedure is obvious.

The bill also allows the courts to order the payment of a provision for costs, declare that a legal action is abusive, condemn a party to pay the fees and extrajudicial costs of the other party, and order a party to pay punitive damages. (Québec 2009)

Do the specific provisions found in this particular law make it possible to achieve these objectives? These have been identified thusly by lawmakers:

- As it is important to promote freedom of expression as affirmed in the Charter of human rights and freedoms;
- As it is important to prevent abusive use of the courts and discourage judicial proceedings designed to thwart the right of citizens to participate in public debate;
- As it is important to promote access to justice for all citizens and to strike a fairer balance between the financial strength of the parties to a legal action. (Québec 2009)

The Quebec law includes a number of interesting features. It is clearly distinguished first of all from the legislative initiatives considered in British Columbia and Nova Scotia by significantly expanding the concept of "abuse" that forms the basis for these legislative models. Under those models, a legal action that hides improper purposes had to exclude any "reasonable" expectation that the final verdict would be favourable to the party that had introduced it and conceal illegitimate extralegal political objectives (that is, dissuade the defendant or other people from participation in public debate, divert the resources of the defendant to the legal dispute or punish the defendant for participating in public debate). The abuse of procedure had to express *improper intentions* associated with and confined to the public participation of its adversary.

The Quebec legislative initiative instead includes, under a single category of "abuse of procedure," a set of procedural infractions indirectly associated with the concept of SLAPP, presented now as a process of diversion of the legal apparatus that limits the freedom of expression of other persons in relation to public debates:

> The procedural impropriety may consist in a claim or pleading that is clearly unfounded, frivolous or dilatory or in conduct that is vexatious or quarrelsome. It may also consist in bad faith, in a use of procedure that is excessive or unreasonable or causes prejudice to another person, or *in*

> *an attempt to defeat the ends of justice, in particular if it restricts freedom of expression in public debate.* (article 54.1., emphasis added)

Thus, the legal changes proposed should not only be applied to strategic lawsuits against public participation — civil lawsuits that constitute a diversion of justice by seeking to muzzle citizen expression and limit public participation — but to a whole set of abusive proceedings currently faced by the Quebec legal system. SLAPPs are therefore understood as a sub-category of co-existing abusive legal proceedings, in particular, ones that are "quarrelsome and frivolous" and not necessarily instigated in response to activities of the defendant. This element represents a major difference with other proposed legislation being studied in Canada.

Law 9 establishes provisions to permit the rapid dismissal of abusive legal proceedings, the awarding of a provision for costs to the defendant (in certain circumstances), the imposition of punitive and exemplary damages to a party that has introduced abusive legal proceedings, the reversal of the burden of proof and the condemnation of the administrators of a legal person that has introduced an abusive legal claim. To do this, this law amends the Quebec Code of Civil Procedure to give additional power to the court so that it can play a more active role in the management of potentially abusive proceedings. Abusive lawsuits, and specifically SLAPPs, are therefore essentially understood as a *procedural* question; the Quebec initiative does not seek to modify the substantive law (and thus create new rights, duties and obligations for the parties),[36] but rather to reorganize the rules of legal disputes to keep one party from instrumentalizing them for illegitimate purposes. Law 9 creates, amends and deletes articles of the Code of Civil Procedure in order to meet this objective.

The mechanism making it possible to fight abusive claims and procedural abuses resides fundamentally in section 54.2[37] of the bill specifying:

> 54.2. If a party establishes that an action or pleading is *prima facie* an abuse of procedure, the onus is on the party who instituted the action or filed the pleading to show that the action or pleading is not an excessive or unreasonable use of procedure and is justified in law.

Defendants who feel that they are victims of an abuse of procedure (and in particular a SLAPP) have to therefore first of all demonstrate summarily that the procedure instigated against them *can* — note here that this criterion is equivalent to a simple possibility, and not to a demonstration — constitute an abuse. When this claim is received, the burden of proof is transferred to the party that instituted the action or filed the pleading: it would have to "show that the action or pleading is not an excessive or unreasonable use of procedure and is justified in law."

When the court has ruled that there is abuse, it can, at its own convenience, "dismiss the action, strike out a submission or require that it be amended, reject a pleading or terminate or refuse to allow an examination" (section 54.3). These provisions are intended to give the court the means necessary to effectively manage the cases in which abuse has been found.

This being said, and specifically because of the problems related to such a finding — abuses in justice are typically far from obvious — the Quebec law gives the court a set of powers that permit it to better manage proceedings in which there is a possibility of abuse. The court will be able to: "subject the furtherance of the action or the pleading to certain conditions" (54.3.1); "require undertakings from the party concerned with regard to the orderly conduct of the proceeding" (54.3.2); "suspend the case for the period it determines" (54.3.3); and "recommend to the chief judge or chief justice that special case management be ordered" (54.3.4). All these measures are aimed, in fact, toward strengthening the control that the judiciary can exercise in order to ensure the smooth conduct of proceedings.

More interestingly (some would say more radically), the Quebec law gives the court the power, when there appears to have been abuse, to order a party that had introduced an action or pleading to pay its adversary a provision for costs — under pain of dismissal of the action or the pleading. A provision for costs is an amount awarded from one party to another, commonly in order to re-establish an economic balance between them and therefore permit the organization of a more equitable legal contest. Under the legislation adopted, the court is able to order the payment of a provision for costs 1) when there appears to be abuse; 2) "if justified by the circumstances"; and 3) "if the court notes that without such assistance the party's financial situation would prevent it from effectively arguing its case" (54.3.5). The essential question, of course, resides in the case law determination of the criteria to establish what constitutes an appearance of abuse, the circumstances justifying the awarding of a provision for costs and, more problematic yet, what is understood by the "financial situation" of a party targeted by a legal action where lacking this assistance "would prevent it from effectively arguing its case."

The good grace and wisdom of the Quebec judiciary will gradually determine if this measure — an unusual procedure in Canadian law — will retain its relevance. In any case, awarding the provision for costs is an effective mechanism to ensure the financial protection of parties targeted by SLAPPs *during* proceedings, something that is frequently lacking in proposed Canadian and American legislation. This measure is also intended to be dissuasive; it can be extremely onerous (and much less attractive) for the SLAPPer to instigate abusive proceedings if it risks having to pay both its own costs and those of its adversaries.

What happens when the court rules that a legal action or a pleading is abusive? The court can first of all order the payment of a provision for costs, condemn a party to pay costs and damages and, "if justified by the circumstances," award punitive damages (section 54.4.). The Quebec law, in accordance with the civil law tradition, gives a certain margin to maneuver to the judiciary so that it can itself determine the appropriate criteria and circumstances for the use of powers for the management of the proceedings entrusted to it. The importance of the preamble included in the

Quebec law is interpretative: it should favour legal interpretations that conform to the aims and objectives defined by the lawmakers. The idea, in other words, was to send a clear signal to the judiciary that they should, in applying the provisions of the legislation, act in a manner compatible with the legislative guidelines.

One of the most appealing provisions in the law — and certainly the most controversial — remains the ability of the court to order administrators and officers of a legal person that have brought improper proceedings to the courts personally to pay damages (section 54.6).[38] This measure is radical in many respects. It removes (theoretically at least) the legal protection enjoyed by company executives who sue, in the name of their corporations, those who oppose their activities or future projects. Ironically, if this procedure is properly used by the courts, it could subject the officers and administrators of corporations to the treatment that they had reserved, remorselessly, for their adversaries.

The application of this provision, however, is not so simple. The measure opens the possibility of a legal mess that could prove to be very complex. Jurisprudence will, here also, determine the relevance and applicability of this innovative measure. To my knowledge, there is no other anti-SLAPP law that includes such a measure.

A Glass Two-Thirds Full

The Quebec anti-SLAPP law should be evaluated as a political statement in that it serves to define the objectives of the justice system. It is therefore aimed not so much at avoiding the judicialization of public debates — although this can have serious consequences on citizen participation — as at preventing abusive attempts to hijack the justice system. While thus limited to strategic lawsuits against public participation, this law also extends to improper actions that do not necessarily have political dimensions; in order to use the provisions that it establishes, it is not necessary to demonstrate to the court a certain form of public participation. Hence the apparent paradox: this legislation, intended essentially as a response by public authorities to a request from Quebec civil society for additional protection for citizens participating in public debate, establishes a much broader legal regime targeting not specifically SLAPPs, but improper claims and proceedings generally.[39]

The law therefore has both a limited and extended scope. Its scope is limited, since it can hardly be applied to cases of gag suits; to take advantage of its provisions, the party that feels it has been the victim of legal intimidation in response to its public participation will have to demonstrate, at the very least, the appearance of abuse — and not simply inhibitory effects on public participation resulting from the proceedings brought against it. For it to be able to intervene, the court will therefore have limit itself to finding "restrictive effects" that inhibit "freedom of expression in public debate," but also and in particular rule on a deliberate attempt to "defeat the ends of justice" or an abuse of process that produces such a result.

We saw this in the previous chapter; the assessment of an anti-SLAPP law is based on four criteria: protection, dissuasive, compensation and punishment. We will review these criteria and examine to what extent the Quebec anti-SLAPP law meets them.[40] Effective protection against SLAPPs assumes both prompt interruption of legal actions undertaken and economic assistance to prevent the financial collapse of the defendant.

Quebec lawmakers refused to hear the demands of civil society groups asking that an expedited process be established in order to ensure the quick hearing of and ruling on motions for the dismissal of proceedings associated with SLAPPs, probably taking the view that the preliminary presentation of these motions would ensure their prompt reception by the courts (see section 54.2., second para.). Until now, and although this is a question of perspective, the law seems to fall short on this precise point. Let us look at the first three rulings that have established case law in the area of SLAPPs in Quebec following adoption of the legislation.[41] The defendants won in all these cases — overall, the Quebec judiciary seems to have understood the message. However, the motions presented by the defendants took an average of about one year before being heard by the courts. That is too long. The legal ordeal of the defendants, as well as the chilling effect of these lawsuits on public debate, is therefore *de facto* permitted to last for months. Certain laws presented in the previous chapter did a better job in this regard.

The Quebec law nevertheless proposes an innovative mechanism to ensure the financial protection of the potential victims of SLAPPs during proceedings. The provision for costs is intended as a kind of financial cushion to mitigate the psychological and financial costs associated with defence and thus relieve the defendant who has not been able to get the lawsuit dismissed (even if the appearance of abuse had been shown successfully) of a potentially crushing burden. The real effectiveness of this measure will be seen in use and according to the jurisprudence that establishes the criteria on the basis of which the courts decide to award such costs.

Does the Quebec law have sufficient strength to discourage potential SLAPPers from using strategies of legal intimidation? It is difficult to say. A few problematic cases have come to light in Quebec since the adoption of the legislation (see, for example, Lalonde 2011).

In June 2009, barely a few days after the adoption of Law 9, citizen Martin Drapeau was sued for $150,000 for damaging the reputation of Constructions Infrabec Inc. This suit resulted from questioning by Mr. Drapeau at a municipal council meeting of the process for awarding a contract for the refurbishment of a water purification plant to the company by the municipality of Boisbriand. Under the new sections introduced into the Code of Civil Procedure, the lawsuit was dismissed and declared abusive by the Quebec Superior Court.[42]

In December 2010, Ugo Lapointe, co-founder and spokesperson of the Coalition pour que le Québec ait meilleure mine! and the newspaper *Le Soleil* received a formal notice demanding that both organizations withdraw statements considered defamatory by the Pétrolia oil company and jointly pay $350,000 to the company in moral and exemplary damages. Interviewed in an article published on

December 3, 2010, in *Le Soleil*, Mr. Lapointe had used the metaphor "theft" to refer to the permission granted to the extractive companies to sell and extract oil and gas resources at the exploration stage without paying royalties to the Quebec government. When the respondents refused to accede to the demands of the company, it brought a lawsuit against them in January 2011. This suit was also ruled abusive and dismissed by the Superior Court.[43]

In August 2011, the Société Radio-Canada announced that it intended to take advantage of the sections included in Law 9 to seek dismissal of a suit instigated against it by Constructions Louisbourg, owned by contractor Tony Accurso. Exceptionally, the lawsuit referred to contempt of court, since Radio-Canada had disseminated information from a file that had been sealed by the courts. The Quebec Superior Court subsequently rejected the accusations of Louisbourg, acquitted the Société Radio-Canada and awarded it costs.[44] Radio-Canada has stated that it was sued on three subsequent occasions after broadcasting reports on Mr. Accurso.[45] It considers therefore "that the action was intended to silence the journalists and prevent the dissemination of new reports on the businesses of Tony Accurso or on himself."[46]

In May 2013, Radio Nord Communications (RCN), the owner of the CHOI Radio X stations, asked the Quebec Superior Court to order the closure of blogs critical of the programming of its stations and brought a lawsuit of $250,000 against Jean-François Jacob, who it considered to be the administrator of these platforms. While he acknowledged having originated a Facebook page critical of CHOI Radio X, Jacob denied being the administrator of the contentious blogs and being behind the movement to boycott the stations. Referred to on these blogs as "trash radio," CHOI Radio X Québec was then targeted by the website sortonslespoubelles.com, of which the aims included alerting advertisers about the kind of things said on the airwaves as well as encouraging Internet users to complain to the Canadian Radio-television and Telecommunications Commission. Jacob was quick to publicly denounce the legal action brought against him, calling it a "gag suit," and a public campaign to support him was organized after he was fired by his employer in response to the lawsuit (Parent 2013, May 25; Duplessis 2013, June 17).

Clearly the adoption of the Quebec anti-SLAPP law has not yet dissuaded the use of the legal system following actions raising questions of public interest. On paper, however, the law includes the essential ingredients for judicial dissuasion: reimbursement of costs, awarding of damages, awarding of punitive damages and, exceptionally, the possibility of personally condemning the administrators of legal persons that have instigated abusive proceedings. The first encouraging sign of the law's dissuasive potential can be seen in the very first case of jurisprudence in the area of SLAPPs in Quebec following the adoption of Law 9, which declared the initial claim "abusive" and therefore dismissed the action of the plaintiff, condemning it to pay $15,000 to the defendant, and awarded the latter the reimbursement of costs.[47]

The possible condemnation of a SLAPPer to reimburse costs and pay damages is intended, of course, as both a dissuasive and compensatory mechanism, but serves additional functions as well. The amount awarded to the victim of judicial abuse is also supposed to properly compensate the defendant for damages suffered. When citizens Serge Galipeau and Christine Landry were finally freed from a claim considered abusive by the courts that had entangled them in a legal web for more than four years, they were disappointed in the reception by the Superior Court of their claim for damages of $578,500 against those who brought the original suit. Although this claim was received favourably by Judge Pierre Dallaire, he ordered only the payment of $142,535 in damages (approximately one quarter of the amount claimed), a sum they considered insufficient to cover the legal costs incurred, compensate for the thousands of hours spent on their defence, as well as to compensate for the anxiety and stress caused by the legal proceedings (Thériault 2011, May 7).

What Should Be Done? Lessons from the Quebec Experience

The relative success of the Quebec anti-SLAPP campaign can be attributed to several factors. The receptivity of politicians to the grievances of civil society groups certainly played a decisive role in the adoption of a law to counteract the phenomenon. However, the first efforts and the rising tide of support for the adoption of the legislation are largely the result of sustained, effective activism. What lessons should be learned from all the hours invested in the organization of an anti-SLAPP struggle in Quebec?

Anti-SLAPP laws touch on sensitive legal issues of access to justice and judicial equality — two closely associated but distinct concepts, which we will look at in the next chapter — and raise difficult questions regarding the balance between the rights of plaintiffs and defendants. Faced with these problems, the proponents of the adoption of an anti-SLAPP law have to convince their fellow citizens, and in particular their elected representatives, of essentially three things:

- The presence of the phenomenon in their jurisdiction — frequently demonstrated using a few cases that have generated media coverage and appreciable mobilization;
- The usefulness or urgency of taking action, either proactively (that is before that the observed phenomenon spreads widely), or correctively; and
- The existence of clear, effective legislative remedies, ideally relatively easy to adopt, that could be applied to correct the situation.

In the absence of one of these three elements, it is likely that the citizens demanding the adoption of legislative measures to curb SLAPPs will meet considerable resistance that could imperil the undertaking. Various strategies can be used to meet these general objectives.

Respond, Escalate, Isolate

Whether it focuses on a specific case or calls for broader legislative reforms, the anti-SLAPP struggle seems to me to be first and foremost a matter of communication.

The Quebec, Canadian, Australian and British experiences show that the groups that have best resisted the legal assaults of their adversaries and inspired appropriate legislative reform are those who have developed the most effective communication strategies.[48] Such strategies must include three basic aspects: response, escalation and political isolation. As we saw in Chapter 2, SLAPPs are based on a principle of a reversal of the offensive and defensive relationships that occur in political disputes. The instigation of legal proceedings against adversaries opposing a filer's actions, projects or ideas typically permits SLAPPers to go from a politically defensive position to a legally offensive position. They should not be permitted this opportunity. It is better, on the contrary, to respond to legal aggression with communications campaigns and launch into a political fight.

In the United Kingdom, for example, David Morris and Helen Steel, two citizens targeted by a lawsuit instituted against them by the fast-food giant McDonald's, transformed the suit into what was subsequently called — to the great displeasure of the multinational — one of the worst public relations disasters in history.[49] At the same time as they were defending themselves in court, these two individuals created a truly national campaign to respond to what they considered to be an obvious attempt at muzzling citizen criticism. The case repeatedly caught the attention the British and international media, which would regularly cover the various developments of the affair.[50] A website <www.mcspotlight.org> containing all the proceedings, processes and documentation related to the case was created, for example. Morris and Steel also made many public statements and gave numerous interviews, and a documentary (*McLibel*) and book (*McLibel: Burger Culture on Trial*, by John Vidal) were produced about these events.

Similar experiences pitting small but vocal Davids against Goliaths have been recorded in various regions of the globe. The communications response to these lawsuits need, in order to be effective, to result in political costs (in terms of image in particular) and economic costs (by affecting revenues and relationships with partners) that are greater than the extralegal gains that the SLAPPer could achieve by continuing with the proceedings against its adversaries. Such a campaign must therefore raise the stakes, pressure the alleged SLAPPer on various fronts and, ideally, isolate it politically. We could look at things this way: SLAPPs can broadly be understood as the abusive and political use of legal proceedings by the actors and categories of actors who possess the sufficient financial and legal capital. They instrumentalize an existing economic imbalance between the parties by converting it into a legal inequality (see the next chapter). The concept of capital — considered here as an asset that can generate benefits — can also be extended to the cultural, social and political spheres. Victims of SLAPPs therefore need to work to erode the social and political capital of their adversaries and generate gains through an effective communications campaign. They have to weaken the networks of support available to their abusers, break economic alliances, counter public relations campaigns and attack their public images. This has been done successfully in Quebec, Canada, Europe, Australia and the United States.

The specific tactics used to do this are up to those who shoulder the campaign; however, a number of general objectives need to be met:

- These efforts need to illustrate the excessive nature of the legal actions;
- They have to show clearly the imbalances that exist between the parties;
- They have to publicly contrast the public interest of the defendants' actions to the private interests (associated with greed and egotism) of the party that has instigated the legal proceedings;
- They have to deal with the human consequences of these actions — and oppose, therefore, the dehumanization associated with legal disputes;
- They have to position the conflict not as a private dispute but as a public issue that determines and defines the limitations of the political rights of a community.

The real danger of these proposed actions is that the misdeeds of activists will serve the cause of the parties that instigated proceedings after public participation by the defendants. Hence the frequent appeal of lawyers to caution and withdrawal. These misdeeds can be made up of verbal offences toward the plaintiffs, the use of language that can be instrumentalized by the opposing party before the courts or the exercise of illegal actions (civil disobedience can, at this stage, antagonize the courts). Caution, therefore, is always a good idea on these questions.

Win Over the Media, Be the Media

The elements presented above can only be relevant to the extent that the actions by the individuals and groups carrying on the anti-SLAPP struggle are effectively directed toward the most strategic public targets. It is therefore necessary to know how to both win over the media and develop effective press skills. This point is crucial. It assumes a precise identification of the various publics that need to be addressed: politicians — and, within each political party, the appropriate contacts — the media (journalists who are aware of and sympathetic to the cause), support networks (on the one hand, the groups and organizations that possess relevant resources and, on the other hand, conscious, mobilized individuals) and the general public — for example, through the Internet.

A process of winning over the media also implies the selection of appropriate spokespersons: this is a crucial element in building the loyalty of media outlets. An effective media strategy is one that meets the needs of the media outlets that will relay the information. Three elements therefore need to be provided to journalists: strong images (in Quebec and Australia, the public display of gags produced these), excerpts ready for use (audio clips, quotations, news releases) and relevant information.

Here are a few suggestions for action:

1. The organization of media events (press conferences, demonstrations, symbolic actions, etc.) to draw the attention of the population to an attempt at legal intimidation;
2. Meetings with local, regional and national elected officials in order to inform them about the existence of the case, to obtain their support and to put the question of SLAPPs onto the legislative agenda;
3. The occasional mobilization of friends, family and ordinary citizens to inform them about the progress of the affair, to plan events, to expand the support network and to establish contacts with citizens and groups who have had similar experiences;
4. Discussions with competent lawyers and efforts to obtain support from the legal community;
5. Information sessions on the risks, impacts and consequences of SLAPPs[51];
6. The maintenance of a strong online presence, including a complete website to archive information related to the issues raised and links to resources and key actors, and the use of social media.[52]

This list is not intended to be exhaustive, but it includes the main actions undertaken by anti-SLAPP activists in Quebec as part of their public activities.

Political Lobbying: Playing with Power

The anti-SLAPP struggle shows the importance of establishing dialogue with all the parties active on the political stage — beyond the affinities or common interests that activists have with certain specific political groups.

There are three reasons for this. First, the most crucial support can come from the least suspected allies. No doors should therefore be closed ahead of time. Second, partisan politics can itself favour advocacy, with parties in power possibly feeling the need to adopt provisions supported publicly by opposition parties, who are trying to gain political capital associated with the anti-SLAPP struggle.

Finally, in most liberal political systems, the legislative initiatives are *de facto* a government prerogative; the legislative agenda is largely determined by the political party in power. It is fundamental to find allies there that can spread discourse and arguments within its political milieu.

As we have seen, the lobbying strategy used by Quebec anti-SLAPP activists is based both on respectful dialogue and constant pressure. It was a matter of developing a social base that would prove useful in negotiations with lawmakers, as they tended to be generally more courteous and attentive when their own political interests were at stake. Finally, the technique of hammering home the message can, under certain conditions, be productive. It is therefore good to repeat the message on every possible tribune.

Anti-SLAPP demonstration in Montreal in 2009. *Photographs by the author.*

Fighting SLAPPs 111

Conclusion

The problem of SLAPPs offers a fruitful avenue for initiating a broader discussion on the role of the law and the legal apparatus in our society. These kinds of lawsuits problematize the ways in which the law seeps into our lives, participates in processes of the construction and definition of social and political problems, and conditions the risks and rewards associated with political participation. The citizens and groups who have asked for legislative reforms have raised such issues: they have criticized the lack of access to and the inequality of the liberal legal system and have deplored the unwarranted judicialization of political controversies. These people have also pressured Quebec lawmakers to admit that the use of the law can pervert and limit the expression of legitimate social and political convictions. This is not insignificant.

Although it has fueled criticism of the flaws in the legal apparatus, the Quebec discourse on SLAPPs has nevertheless revolved around an essentially reformist perspective: it was much more a matter of proposing compensatory mechanisms targeted toward rectifying the failures of this apparatus than of calling into question the processes at the root of the problem, namely the inordinate expansion of the law outside the courts and intrusion of capitalist relationships into the legal system. We will look at this thorny issue in the next chapter.

Notes

1. For a more extensive presentation of the various stages that have marked the anti-SLAPP mobilization in Quebec, see Lemonde and Ferland-Gagnon 2010 and Landry 2010.
2. Although officially launched on October 10, 2006, the campaign *Citoyens, taisez-vous!* [Citizens, Keep Quiet!] nevertheless began informally many months earlier. The people from the AQLPA had been working since March 2006 to put the issue of SLAPPs in Quebec on the public political agenda. This effort was marked by the organization of press conferences on the experiences of the citizens and organizations that had been sued, by writing letters to newspapers and by political lobbying to convince lawmakers to act. The launch of the *Citoyens, taisez-vous!* campaign gave an official name to the lobbying, solidarity and grassroots education efforts on SLAPPs and would generate extensive media attention on these activities.
3. The website of the campaign <http://www.taisez-vous.org/> originally contained a vast quantity of information on the dispute between the CRRE and the AQLPA and their adversary. This information would be withdrawn when an out-of-court settlement was negotiated between the parties in December 2007. However, the website remained active and provided an information base during public hearings on SLAPPs that took place before a parliamentary commission in 2008.
4. This shift in leadership can be explained both by the financial and human exhaustion of the members of the AQLPA, who then refocused their work on their initial environmental activities (and therefore avoided the bankruptcy of the organization), and by the development of a broad Quebec anti-SLAPP coalition. The AQLPA would nevertheless remain a key player in the coalition.
5. The lawsuits targeting Serge Galipeau and Christine Landry, and the one against

6. The president of AQLPA, André Bélisle, declared at the launch of the campaign: "What is happening to us now represents a dangerous precedent that threatens freedom of expression and what is now called citizen participation, one of the foundations of democratic life…. The Quebec government must act and ensure that the judiciary is given the power to quickly dismiss such unfounded lawsuits. The government must give its citizens the right to express themselves on issues that are important to their community." Association québécoise de lutte contre la pollution atmosphérique (AQLPA) and the Comité de restauration de la Rivière Etchemin (CRRE), *Citoyens, taisez-vous! — Campagne de mobilisation contre les poursuites abusives : Plusieurs dizaines de groupes sociaux, centrales syndicales, partis politiques et artistes appuient deux groupes environnementaux poursuivis injustement*, October 10, 2006, <http://www.aqlpa.com/communiques-de-aqlpa.html?start=22>.
7. This request was formulated in a news release by PQ MNAs Stéphane Bédard, then spokesperson of the official opposition on justice, and Stéphane Tremblay, spokesperson on the environment. In their news release, dated September 15, 2006, the MNAs declared: "the official opposition feels that the government of Quebec should quickly indicate what its intentions are and how it intends to act to prevent the use of such a procedure that can infringe on rights to freedom of expression" (Bédard and Tremblay 2006).
8. Thirty-eight groups and citizens submitted briefs during these public consultations. Thirty of these groups spoke before the Commission. Among those, twenty-two made presentations on the question of SLAPPs, while the others talked exclusively about reform of the Code of Civil Procedure, which was also discussed during these exchanges.
9. Moreover the political lobbying work was not limited to the Minister of Justice. Various members of opposition parties were contacted individually by the members of the anti-SLAPP coalition to ensure their support for an eventual bill and induce the minister to act on the issue.
10. However, the real start for this coalition had occurred a few months earlier with the organization of a first public education meeting on SLAPPs in Montreal. This meeting, organized by the Réseau québécois des groupes écologistes in partnership with the community service department of UQAM, brought together about thirty individuals from various Quebec community groups. Three of the main organizations that would eventually be the mainstays of the Quebec anti-SLAPP campaign — the AQLPA, the Quebec Civil Liberties Union and the Réseau québécois des groupes écologistes — established their first contacts at this meeting.
11. The formal notice stated in particular: "Reading the promotional materials distributed on the website of Écosociété leaves no doubt that this book contained false and highly defamatory allegations about Barrick…. Let there be no doubt that Barrick will demand, among other things, substantial damages against each of the individuals covered by this letter, jointly and severally, as well as any injunction required to put a stop to all defamatory behaviour toward it." The text of this notice was taken from the site <slapp/ecosociete.org>, consulted in June 2011. This site is now closed.
12. However, a "non-launch," that is, a public event discussing the issues of the book and the legal reasons why it was not being launched, was organized and attracted the attention of the media and the general public.

13. See, for example, Écosociété, "Attaque à la liberté d'expression: Écosociété est l'objet de deux SLAPP," <slapp.ecosociete.org/fr/node/65>. See also Radio-Canada 2008, May 6.
14. The motion to institute proceedings stipulated in particular: "The Defendants have engaged in a carefully orchestrated and unlawful campaign of defamation against Barrick. Their campaign of defamation has been carried on in Quebec and elsewhere in Canada and they intend to extend it to Europe. The defendants have planned, orchestrated and implemented their campaign of defamation against Barrick with malice, for the express purposes of publicly embarrassing Barrick, of maximizing to the extent possible the publication and re-publication of their false statements against Barrick, of harming Barrick's reputation and of injuring Barrick in its business and trade." (Quoted from *Motion to institute proceedings and a permanent injunction: Barrick Gold v. Les Éditions Écosociété inc., Alain Deneault, William Sacher & Delphine Abadie*, 2008.)
15. The defence of Éditions Écosociété was provided both by lawyers supplied by the insurers of the publisher and a legal team working mostly on a *pro bono* basis led, among others, by Normand Tamaro.
16. See "Barrick Gold déclare des profits records de 837 millions US," <lapresseaffaires.cyberpresse.ca>, October 28, 2010.
17. Pierre Noreau, coauthor of the expert report commissioned by the Minister of Justice, also offered his support to the organization. See the petition available online: *Threats Against Freedom of Expression and Academic Freedom by Canadian Companies*: <http://www.freespeechatrisk.ca/academic-petition/>.
18. Gabrielle Ferland-Gagnon has provided a thorough, precise record of the efforts carried out jointly by the members of the Quebec anti-SLAPP coalition.
19. A press conference organized jointly by the RQGE, Éditions Écosociété, the Quebec Civil Liberties Union and the AQLPA was, for example, held on June 11, 2008, on the steps of the Montreal courthouse. The media event was intended to push lawmakers to introduce an anti-SLAPP bill before the end of the parliamentary session. Twenty-three organizations took part in the public event and agreed to gag themselves in front of the courthouse to draw the attention of the media — and incidentally the legislator — to the urgency of adopting a law to deal with the problem of SLAPPs in Quebec.
20. The anti-SLAPP coalition then sent out a news release to the media to express their partial satisfaction with the bill and their concerns regarding some of its provisions. The absence of an emergency procedure permitting the quick hearing and dismissal of SLAPPs, the restrictive nature of the financial protection that could be granted to SLAPP victims, the absence of precision on the application of provisions of the law to pending causes and the lack of provisions to deal with the problem of the gag clauses that are found in out-of-court settlements in SLAPP cases were considered limitations of the bill.
21. The members of the anti-SLAPP coalition took advantage of the greater availability of sitting MNAs, now freed of their parliamentary responsibilities, to lobby and consult with key players in the opposition parties.
22. The Quebec Bar, while reaffirming its doubts about the need for legislation, suggested modifications to improve the bill. The analysis of this proposal leads me nevertheless to think this was intended to gut the bill and remove its most relevant provisions. See Quebec Bar 2008.
23. Confédération des syndicats nationaux 2008; ATTAC-Québec 2008; Association

québécoise de lutte contre la pollution atmosphérique et Comité de restauration de la rivière Etchemin 2008.

24. The text of letter read: "Whereas that there is a broad consensus in Quebec about the protection of freedom of expression, whereas the three parties sitting in the National Assembly are in favour of this bill and whereas another minority government could be elected, which could result in the death of a second bill, we ask the spokespersons on justice of the three main parties to present, at the very beginning of the next session, a motion to resume consideration of Bill 99 at the stage where it was when the 1st session of the 38th legislature was dissolved," RQGE, Quebec Civil Liberties Union, AQLPA and Éditions Écosociété 2008.

25. The election was won by the Liberal Party, which went from a minority mandate to a majority mandate. Jacques Dupuis was named parliamentary leader of the government and gave up his former ministerial functions. Katherine Weil, a newcomer in Quebec politics, became Minister of Justice. Parti Québécois became the official opposition, replacing Action démocratique du Québec. Parti Québécois MNA Daniel Turp lost his seat in Mercier to Amir Khadir of Québec solidaire. Véronique Hivon replaced Daniel Turp as Parti Québécois spokesperson on justice. Claude L'Écuyer also lost his seat in Saint-Hyacinthe as part of a sharp decline in support for the Action démocratique du Québec party.

26. A copy of Law 9 can be found as an appendix.

27. Nevertheless, efforts made by the Quebec Civil Liberties Union and the Réseau québécois des groupes écologistes to inform the Quebec population about the provisions of Law 9 should be mentioned. Following adoption of the law, these groups did a tour of Quebec and presented in various assemblies both the issue of SLAPPs and the mechanisms that had been put in place in Quebec to fight them.

28. See "Loi sur les poursuites abusives," *L'Aut'Journal* (source: Écosociété), June 4, 2009. <http://www.lautjournal.info/default.aspx?page=3&NewsId=1644>.

29. *Barrick Gold Corporation c. Éditions Écosociété inc.* 2011 QCCS 4232, para. 30. Translation.

30. *Barrick Gold Corporation c. Éditions Écosociété inc.* 2011 QCCS 4232, para. 25 et 30. Translation.

31. A team of legal experts, for example, defended the actions against Éditions Écosociété and the authors of *Noir Canada* at a parliamentary commission during the special consultations on Bill 99 in October 2008.

32. *Barrick Gold Corporation c. Éditions Écosociété inc.* 2011 QCCS 4232, para. 17. Translation.

33. "Fin de la poursuite de Barrick Gold: Écosociété règle hors cour," CNW, October 18, 2011. <www.newswire.ca/fr/story/860811/fin-de-la-poursuite-de-barrick-gold-ecosociete-regle-hors-cour>.

34. The publisher also insisted that it would not modify its publishing choices following these lawsuits. For example, it published the book *Paradis sous terre* [Paradise under Earth], a book by Iain Deneault and William Sacher on the same subject as *Noir Canada*, as well as the original French version of this book.

35. See *Barrick Gold Corporation c. Éditions Écosociété inc.* 2011 QCCS 4232.

36. This procedural approach is distinguished from the legislative initiative in New Brunswick, which defines a right of participation in the affairs of government, and from the British Columbia initiative, which gave qualified privilege in the area of

defamation to actors who have engaged in legitimate public participation.
37. The numbers mentioned in the bill correspond to the sections of the Code of Civil Procedure that came into effect after the adoption of Law 9 by the National Assembly.
38. The section in question reads as follows: "54.6. If the abuse of procedure is committed by a legal person or a person who acts as the administrator of the property of another, the directors and officers of the legal person who took part in the decision or the administrator of the property of another may be personally condemned to pay damages."
39. Nevertheless, and the legislator was very rigorous in this regard, the wording of the legislation clearly suggests that it should be applied for the protection of rights and freedoms and of citizen participation in public debates.
40. The assessment presented here is based among other things on a previously published article. See Landry 2010.
41. See *Constructions Infrabec inc. c. Drapeau*, QCCS 1734, 2010; 2332 4197 Québec inc. c. Galipeau, QCCS 3427, 2010; *Trace Foundation c. Centre for Research on Globalization (CRG)*, QCCS 2119, 2010.
42. See *Constructions Infrabec inc. c. Drapeau* QCCS 1734, 2010.
43. See *3834310 Canada inc. & Ugo Lapointe c. Pétrolia inc.*, 200-17-014133-Q10.
44. *Constructions Louisbourg ltée c. Société Radio-Canada*, 2012 QCCS 767.
45. The lawsuit was dismissed on March 1, 2012, by Judge Jean-Pierre Sénécal, who emphasized in his verdict the obvious public interest of this case. See also *Accurso v. Gravel*, 2011 QCCS 158 (CanII).
46. See Société Radio-Canada 2011, August 24.
47. See *Constructions Infrabec inc. c. Drapeau*, QCCS 1734, 2010.
48. I hope I have been able to illustrate this point using the cases involving the Association québécoise de lutte contre la pollution atmosphérique, the Friends of the Lubicon and Gunns 20.
49. The bad publicity surrounding the affair is said to have, among other things, persuaded the company to try to settle out of court with the defendants, who twice refused the terms presented to them. See <www.mcspotlight.org/case/trial/story.html>.
50. The court hearings lasted a total of 313 days, from June 28, 1994, to December 16, 1996. The case was eventually appealed, then brought before the European Court of Human Rights. There, the final verdict, rendered in February 2005, would bring an end to more than fifteen years of legal wrangling opposing primarily two citizens and a restaurant multinational, and then the British government.
51. The Ligue des droits et libertés and the Réseau québécois des groupes écologistes do remarkable work in this area in Quebec.
52. This section has been adapted from Landry, Normand, "La parole citoyenne SLAPée," Office national du film du Canada: Parole citoyenne, 2009 <parolecitoyenne.org/sites/citoyen.onf.ca/files/slapp_12.pdf>.

Chapter 5

SLAPPs as a Symptom

Despite their negative effects, SLAPPs provide an opportunity for a fascinating — and necessary — reflection on the role of the law and the legal system in our society. Such a reflection sheds new light on the way in which they worm their way into our lives, play a role in the processes of construction and definition of social and political issues, and influence the risks and rewards associated with participation in public affairs.

The practices of intimidation and legal repression presented in this book occur in a context marked by the growing use of the courts in social and political conflicts and the exacerbation of deep inequalities in the area of justice. These practices capitalize on the affirmation of a centre of legal power being used to manage, regulate and administer citizen participation in public debate. They also show how economic influences have seeped into the legal system and into the role it plays in the dynamics of political domination. In short, these practices highlight the profoundly inequitable nature of a legal process that subjects political participation to a logic of control and management.

This is an essential discussion, but it is largely absent from debates on SLAPPs, and it still needs to take place. This chapter will examine strategic lawsuits against public participation as an indicator of social and political dysfunctions, produced by a phenomenon of contamination of our society by the law and its associated processes. Through an analysis of the repercussions of the growing numbers of restrictive rules used to discipline public debate, SLAPPs need to be studied in the context of an inequitable, unequal capitalist political economy of justice.

The Judicialization of Public Debates

About two centuries ago, Alexis de Tocqueville, a key figure in political liberalism, declared:

> There is hardly any political question in the United States that sooner or later does not turn into a judicial question. From that, the obligation that the parties find in their daily polemics to borrow ideas and language from the judicial system. Since most public men are or have formerly been jurists, they make the habits and the turn of ideas that belong to jurists pass into the handling of public affairs. The jury ends up by familiarizing all classes with them. Thus, judicial language becomes, in

> a way, the common language; so the spirit of the jurist, born inside the schools and courtrooms, spreads little by little beyond their confines; it infiltrates all of society, so to speak; it descends to the lowest ranks, and the entire people finishes by acquiring a part of the habits and tastes of the magistrate. (Tocqueville 2010: 441)

This insightful analysis also holds true for Canada in the twenty-first century. The inclusion of a national charter of rights and freedoms in the 1982 Constitution helped to speed up the process that had already begun to affirm legal power in the country and favour a redefinition of Canadian citizenship around specific legal principles (see Monton 2002; Clément 2008; Ignatieff 2000). The legal system is now deeply integrated within Canadian political life.

Law, Rights and Legal Power

While it is expressed most clearly inside the courts, the law also contributes to the articulation of social and political discourse in the public sphere. Appeals to rights, common in public controversies, allow stakeholders to express grievances using meaningful concepts and to favour the political participation of marginalized and persecuted groups. This participation is moreover now referred to essentially in terms of *rights* — right to freedom of expression, right to participation in public affairs, right to equality, right to a healthy environment — and in keeping with *the law*: the form of political participation that is considered legitimate is endorsed by the government and subject to official rules governing acceptable conduct.

The result of successive processes of education and consciousness-raising about fundamental rights that have occurred in Canada over recent decades has led to the development of a *rights culture* that is now an integral part of our social and political life. The national community is now seen as a group of people who have rights, who aware of and want to affirm those rights, and who look at complex social relationships in terms of rights.[1]

The gradual affirmation of a rights culture in the country undeniably represents democratic progress, and it has contributed to positioning the human individual as a subject who has intrinsic value and not just as a common object of governance. It has helped to limit, control and prevent the use of force and arbitrary constraint by the state — and, increasingly, by other agents of power — against vulnerable subjects. This rights culture has also fueled the formation of movements demanding that the government intervene in the social, economic and cultural domains in order to ensure the effective enjoyment of specific rights.[2]

> This is the background against which we must set the Canadian Charter — a world that increasingly accepts that legislators may properly be limited by the need to conform to certain basic norms — norms of democracy, norms of individual freedoms like free expression and association, norms governing the legal process by which the state can

deprive people of their liberty and security, and norms of equal treatment. (McLachlin 2009: 64)

The inclusion of the Canadian *Charter of Rights and Freedoms* in the *Constitution Act* of 1982 did nevertheless favour what some call "judicial activism" by the courts, since they are asked to play a significantly broader, sometimes proactive, role in the formulation of public policies.[3] Social and political questions are increasingly referred to in legal language based on the concept of rights — the preserve of the judiciary. Armed with the Charter, of which it is guarantor and final interpreter, the Supreme Court of Canada is called upon to oversee, advise and invalidate the work of legislators as well as intervene, sometimes proactively, in the processes that determine the public interest.[4] This expanded role of the courts, judges and lawyers in the political affairs of the country is regularly associated with the threat of the subordination of politics to the judiciary and the gradual obsolescence of the Canadian parliamentary system (as well as the concept of public debate) in favour of technocracy and legal authoritarianism (see Knopff and Morton 1992). Not everyone has shown the same enthusiasm about the inclusion of a Canadian *Charter of Rights and Freedoms* in the Constitution, which consolidated the role of the legal system in the political life of the country. Russell, for example, argued that the Charter represents a "flight from politics, a deepening disillusionment with the procedures of representative government and government by discussion as means of resolving fundamental questions of political justice" (Russell 1982: 32).

Thirty years after the adoption of the Charter, the Canadian courts now have to be viewed as *judicial legislators* who cooperate with political lawmakers and sometimes oppose them. Legal language, discourse and norms now seep into and restrict political disputes; the very process of bargaining, negotiation, communication, and the combining of forces and interests that characterize politics is placed in a position of competition and cooperation with a formal, procedural legal process. The courts profoundly restrain and restrict political debate, both within parliamentary institutions and in the broader and more diverse public space. In countries that have entrenched rights and freedoms in their constitutions, the essential question is how to circumscribe the work of the courts so that they do not come to dominate political discussions.

Power, as Foucault (1975) says, is a productive, dynamic creature: it gets things done as much as it prohibits, it encourages behaviours and favours specific actions. The increase in judicial power in Canada and elsewhere in the world obliges various social and political actors to abandon a public space of political discussion and to refocus their activities within a judicial apparatus that is now imposing itself as an indispensable arena of social and political struggle. This phenomenon, which can be described using the concept of the judicialization of public debates, is part of the trend that has been observed of the mobilization of the legal system to settle the disputes that occur in social life, as well as the transformation of political controversies into legal disputes.

This phenomenon is evocative of a reflex, more and more widespread, to refer to and deal with social and political problems in terms of rights (and not of choices) requiring that judges be addressed (and not the men and women occupying elective offices) for the formulation of grievances and demands concerning social problems expressed in legal (and not political) language. Such a process favours the obsolescence of discussion, negotiation and political logic in favour of the application or formulation of authoritarian legal norms. Rather than debating, you plea; rather than convincing, you stipulate the legal standard; rather than negotiating, you impose. This raises serious problems of political philosophy. These intrusions of the law are considered by certain philosophers and intellectuals as a veritable legal pollution leading to the bureaucratization of the social world and the colonization of human relationships by a logic and set of norms not suited to them (Teubner 1987). The law conquers, regulates and governs constantly more territory (a phenomenon of the expansion of the law), perpetually subdivides and specializes (a phenomenon of the densification of the law); its expansion represents an increasing domestication of social relationships by formal and authoritarian norms hostile to compromise, dialogue and accommodation. The instrumental logic characteristic of the bureaucratic processes of the governance of the state also perpetually seeps further into the domains of daily life, spontaneous interactions and political discussion, which it gradually smothers.

The judicialization of public debates can be divided into two specific processes: the instrumentalization of the coercive power of the rule of law to circumvent or defeat resistance encountered in the public sphere, and the use of the rules governing legal disputes in order to impose oneself politically.

The Appropriation of the Binding Rule

Legal norms are binding rules. "The rule of law is sanctioned by constraint — this is a specific characteristic of the rule of law. A rule that is not mandatory would not be a rule of law" (Mazeaud et al. 1972: 24–25). Transgression of the rules, conventions and principles governed by the law permits the state to sanction wrongdoing.[5] The tacit threat of humiliation and repression thus encourages the litigant to submit.

A public debate is judicialized when stakeholders turn to the courts to achieve dominance on a controversial question in public space (see Silverstein 2009). The plaintiff thus entrusts the judiciary with deciding on a contentious question (right to abortion, marriage between same-sex couples, death penalty, etc.) and hopes to use the legal process as a lever to win the political fight taking place outside the courts.

The legal norm, which is binding and carries sanctions, can therefore be imposed, produced, reformulated or instrumentalized within the framework of public debates. Participants in public debates have four options for the judicialization of issues:

1. The imposition of the legal norm. This option is the application of constraint through the rule of law. For actors involved in a political conflict, this means demonstrating before a court that practices, actions or omissions by their adversaries contravene the law, in order to subject them to corrective measures or halt their activities. The courts regularly receive applications from, for example, environmental groups to block or delay controversial industrial projects. These groups commonly bring up non-compliance with environmental laws or procedural and bureaucratic faults (related to obtaining permits, the holding of public consultations, etc.).
2. The creation of the legal norm. This option is that of the creation of law. By entrusting the judiciary to decide a socially or politically controversial issue, the litigant permits the legal apparatus to establish norms that distinguish the behaviours endorsed and protected by the state from those that deserve to be punished. The Supreme Court of Canada has determined, for instance, that the constitutional protection of freedom of expression applies to commercial expression and has thus invalidated a Quebec law making French the exclusive language of commercial signage in the province.[6] By identifying the question of commercial signage with freedom of expression, the Supreme Court created a standard that has a significant impact on the linguistic policies of Quebec — a key issue in the political life of the province. The use of the courts makes it possible to create norms that have profoundly political dimensions.
3. Reformulation. This option is that of the rewriting of the law. The ambiguities of the law and its many contradictions offer opportunities for politically active citizens, politicians or groups to obtain from the courts reformulations of specific norms and judgments that coincide better with their positions or interests (Merry 1990). The Supreme Court of Canada, for example, ruled in 2002 that secondary picketing is not illicit, contradicting certain decisions by lower courts and upholding others.[7] By doing so, it reformulated and clarified a profoundly political norm related to the right of employees to demonstrate on sites other than their work sites. While it is circumscribed by jurisprudence, this process of rewriting the law by courts in relationship to public debates permits social and political actors to renegotiate legal norms and alter power relations.
4. The strategic instrumentalization of judicial procedure. This option is that of the capture of the judicial procedure. The instrumentalization of the rules governing legal disputes can give a powerful advantage to public stakeholders by:

    a. *Forcing the inclusion of parties refusing to engage in public debate.* This offensive strategy is intended to force adversaries who are fleeing the debate back into the public arena to deal with contentious questions by bringing lawsuits. In the United States, the question of pay equity was dealt with before the courts after employers refused to enter into dialogue on the issue (McCann 1994).

b. *Excluding parties from political discussions.* This strategy, defensive in nature, is intended to reduce the number and influence of adversaries faced by actors participating in public debate. By suing certain of their adversaries, that is, by reformulating their political grievances in legal language, the plaintiff partially *privatizes* the initial conflict and excludes the actors that have not been cited as parties to the lawsuit. This process makes it possible to transfer a social or political battle that has few chances of being won in the public space into the legal arena and to provide an enclave of relative safety for stakeholders facing difficulties in the political sphere. It thus becomes attractive for the representatives of minority groups to undertake legal proceedings that will lead to the development or imposition of norms the application of which will be ensured by the repressive apparatus of the state. This kind of process has, for example, been undertaken in the United States in relationship to the polarized debates on induced abortions.

c. *Imposing the burden of defence on adversaries.* The conduct of legal disputes is onerous and can produce negative publicity for one or more of the parties involved. A lawsuit (or the threat of a lawsuit) in relationship to public controversies can therefore encourage accommodations, openness and political negotiation (McCann 1994). This strategy is used against corporations or political figures who do not want to see their action examined by the courts or against adversaries who do not possess the necessary resources for the conduct of an extended legal dispute.

The four options presented above bear witness to the increasing use of the law and the legal apparatus in relationship to public debates. They show a willingness that can be observed, on both sides, to rearticulate political discourse in a legal form and mobilize legal proceedings to impose one's will politically in the public space.

SLAPPs are very much part of this trend, representing its extreme manifestation. They belong to a logic of strategic instrumentalization of legal proceedings and show an increasingly widespread desire among public stakeholders to control the spectrum of public debate, to select specific adversaries and interlocutors, and to impose on them strict rules to define and circumscribe discussions.

Like any form of judicialization of public debates, SLAPPs lead to the formalization of disputes between political adversaries: the arena is clearly and carefully defined (the court), the rules that govern the presentation of arguments are procedural and restrictive (legal proceedings), and sanctions await the party found to be at fault. More than anything, SLAPPs indicate the general trend toward the privatization of public debates, with the rejection of political dialogue in favour of a strict concept of individual rights brandished reflexively during public controversies.

Understood this way, phenomena involving the judicialization of public debates, which include SLAPPs, are manifestations of a logic of management, control and supervision of social and political conflicts taken to the extreme, sustained by an expanding legal apparatus. Anti-SLAPP and anti-gag legislative provisions, whether in Quebec, Canada or in other jurisdictions, all have the objective, to use the terminology of German philosopher Jürgen Habermas, of building "a democratic dam against the colonizing encroachment" (and I add) of a legal system that interferes with — or even circumvents — processes of social and political discussion that take place in the public sphere (Habermas 1992: 444). The most effective anti-SLAPP and anti-gag legislative initiatives are unquestionably those that create zones of "dejudicialization"" or "non-judicialization" of public debates, that reject the transformation of controversies into legal disputes at the expense of public debate, which is fundamental in democracy. Legislation should therefore have the objective to "avoid having these divergences of opinions between the parties be uselessly judicialized" and to "return as quickly as possible" the discussions under debate to a political arena.[8]

Disciplining Public Debate

SLAPPs make necessary a critical evaluation of the increasingly wide influence of the domain of the law and its associated processes outside of the legal sphere; they also call for an analysis of the consequences of the increasing number of legal constraints that control political life.

This control is most directly applied in the domain of public debate. A set of authoritarian, extremely technical norms now govern citizen participation in public affairs, distinguishing healthy, legitimate participation (endorsed by the state) from reprehensible political actions (sanctioned by the state), and dictating the nature of acceptable conduct. The right to reputation — very broad in Quebec and in Canada (see Trudel 2007, July 19) — is therefore used to control citizen communications by defining areas of state non-protection and intolerance, opening the way to the legal repression of communications considered illegitimate.

The pitfalls associated with political participation thus include the risk of a regression of political discourse into communications strictly compatible with the rule of law and minimizing the risks of a forced displacement to the legal arena. These can lead to the refinement of public discourse into juridically acceptable and legally safe formats (therefore reducing the risks of a movement to and an entanglement in the legal arena). Public stakeholders are thus induced to formulate their discourse *strategically* rather than *morally*, that is, in a way that expresses convictions in relation to what they consider just and desirable.

What is more, the growing danger of seeing oneself dragged into a slow, onerous and foreign arena obliges the conscientious citizen to think like a lawyer.

This point perhaps constitutes the most pernicious aspect of the phenomenon: the inclusion of legal contingencies in social and political debates taking place *outside* the legal system. This situation is similar to the legal colonization of public debates, which constitutes a powerful tool of censorship that weakens, distorts and hinders citizen political participation *even though it is established and protected by the law*. The appearance of the figure of the prudent, calculating and moderate activist lawyer makes us wary of the spectre of a clamp-down on dissidence by a legal apparatus that sanctions — sometimes severely — errors in law, whether they are intentional or not.

The SLAPP is a concrete manifestation of such a problem. It appears in the North American context as an opportunity that could be seized by the actors who possess a high level of legal and financial capital — and more specifically corporations, promoters and merchants — to respond through legal avenues to the extensive political and media influence of civil society groups. It is used to capitalize on the increased discipline exerted by the law on citizen participation in public debate in order to oblige public stakeholders to exercise caution and restraint. The fear provoked by the judicial process is now enough to discipline social and political life.

Legal Inequality, Political Domination

Officially, the primary function of the legal system is to render justice. This task is laborious. It requires the interpretation of the law, the jurisprudence and the lawmakers' intentions. It necessitates the hearing of complex conflicts and the management of proceedings to ensure both respect for the rights of the parties and the sound conduct of proceedings. Finally it implies the judgment and evaluation of cases on substance, and the consideration of the rights, duties and obligations of the parties — between each other and toward the state, the guarantor of public order.

A healthy, inclusive justice system requires the combination of two aspects that are both distinct and closely associated: an *equitable legal process* and an *enlightened, impartial verdict*. A sound court ruling will first of all be the outcome of a legal process that ensures the parties equitable treatment. The proceedings should be conducted promptly and effectively, by limiting administrative unwieldiness, costs, constraints and delays. Inefficient justice is disparaged justice.[9] Legal entanglements, which are usual in complex cases, do great harm to justice. The legal proceedings should therefore avoid favouring one party to the detriment of another; the rules governing legal disputes should be neutral in their effects and ensure the smooth conduct of the cases brought before the courts. The principle of judicial equity contrasts with the economic inequalities that favour wealthier individuals and groups.

The court ruling given at the end of this process must offer a pertinent analysis of the rights and duties of the parties, free of outside influences,[10] as well as the biases, preferences, and political and ideological convictions of the judges themselves. An impartial, enlightened verdict is based on the rule of law and does not deviate from it; other considerations should (theoretically) be excluded. When all is said and done, an enlightened, legitimate verdict assumes logic, reflection, judgment, deduction and analysis. It happens regularly — and the appeal courts exist expressly for this reason — that judges err in their decisions. The hierarchical organization of our legal system favours the review of decisions made by lower courts and thus permits the correction of erroneous judgments.

SLAPPs have an essential educational function of revealing clearly the permanence of structural inequalities within the legal system. They expose its failings to provide ordinary citizens with full, equitable access to the bodies charged with hearing and managing legal cases: they bear witness, by their very existence, to the inequitable and inefficient nature of legal proceedings, which can be subject to economic influences. In short, SLAPPs highlight the social and political repercussions of the privatization of the costs associated with legal representation and the settlement of disputes before the courts. Two factors are involved: unequal access to justice, resulting essentially from the costs associated with the legal process and lawyers' fees, and inequitable legal disputes favouring actors who possess the capital required for full legal representation of their interests.

Access to Justice

The question of the accessibility of justice remains without a doubt one of the most thorny problems faced by our legal system.[11] It is usually presented as the result of procedural overloading that corrupts the legal system, chronic underfunding of the legal system by the government, thresholds of eligibility for legal aid that are low and unsatisfactory, and an inefficient and archaic organization of justice. Without a doubt, these are important factors. Yet, the perspective proposed here differs: the lack of access to justice seems to me to be primarily the consequence of an abdication by the state of its fundamental responsibilities in the area of justice.

Access to the legal system and to legal representation has significant financial barriers. In Quebec, the average hourly rate charged by a lawyer in a civil law case in 2008 was 171 dollars (*Protégez-vous* 2009: 39). Access to legal representation services thus means, for the average litigant, the rapid depletion of his or her assets and the borrowing of substantial sums of money. Lawyers' fees are not, however, the only costs incurred. Cases dragging on, the extreme technicality of the legal system and the many recurrent, related costs will finally drain the capital of litigants.

The Quebec judiciary has expressed surprise and regret about a growing number of litigants appearing before the courts without lawyers; this phenomenon highlights the prohibitive nature of the costs associated with legal representation. It shows that the current use of private capital by those who enter the legal arena makes access to the courts dependent on the solvency of applicants. The problem of the accessibility of justice is thus, first of all, a problem of the privatization of the costs associated with legal representation and the legal process. This privatization of costs goes against a concept of justice as an essential public service that is supposed to be universal. It gives those that possess capital privileged access to an arena that less wealthy individuals and groups avoid. SLAPPs rely on this inequality and reveal a model of access to justice that is configured institutionally to favour the representation of the interests of capital:

> The quest for equal access for all to legal services goes back to the very foundation of states and juxtaposes both charitable concepts, such as the choice of certain lawyers to take on causes without being paid, and the intention to ensure for a defined class of the community legal services directly in line with the very concept of a society of law. However, it was only in the twentieth century that there have been efforts to establish public and collective systems to ensure access to justice for the poor. Thus, the United States, the United Kingdom and Canada went from the charitable form to more complete regimes entirely funded by the state. (Groupe de travail sur la révision du régime d'aide juridique au Québec 2005: 5)

This quest for "equal access for all" is paradoxically carried out within the framework of a private free market of legal representation, which remains antithetical to distributive paradigms of equality. It goes without saying that the *natural* relationship between a litigant and a lawyer is a commercial one: it is standard that access to services of legal representation is in accordance with the financial resources available to the person using them. Since the distribution of capital in capitalist societies is fundamentally unequal, access to the legal system is inevitably affected.

Although they have achieved significant gains in promoting justice equality, the current access to justice regimes[12] can only partially compensate for the failures of the market generated by the current organization of the supply of legal representation, which favours the transfer of social and economic inequalities to the legal arena. The full correction of this inequality would require a significantly increased socialization of the costs associated with access to the legal system and the establishment of a universal public legal representation service. It is very unlikely that such action will be taken any time soon in Quebec or elsewhere in Canada. In the absence of a real political will to attack the root of the problem of accessibility of justice, anti-SLAPP laws seek to bring to an end as quickly as possible an unaffordable judicial process and provide a form of financial protection for the victims of legal intimidation. They thus make it easier to live with the dysfunctions produced by an inequitable justice system.

Inequitable Justice

Unequal access to the courts constitutes the primary and major inequality in the area of justice. To this is added a structural bias — because it is part of the very way the justice system operates — maintained by the legal system in favour of actors who possess the capital required for the legal representation of their interests.

It seems that the current configuration of justice permits, and in large part favours, processes that transform economic inequalities into judicial inequalities. The actors who possess the capital required for legal representation enjoy greater access to the legal system, better legal expertise, more complete preparation of their case and a greater capacity to pay the costs — financial, temporal, psychological — associated with the conduct of a legal dispute. This predominance encourages the instrumentalization of legal proceedings to drain the resources of an adversary and exhaust him or her financially and psychologically. The party who possesses greater resources can use more and more claims, examinations and expertise at the expense of adversaries who do not possess the financial resources to respond in an equivalent way. This fact is well known; it is tolerated by the judicial and political elites, who prefer adapting to it and formulating palliative — and largely unsatisfactory — responses at the margins of the problem rather than attacking it head-on. The inequitable nature of the judicial process results from the development of capitalist relations at the very heart of the apparatus charged with rendering justice.

Legal equality, it is said, is to the legal domain what universal suffrage is to the political domain (see Noreau 2005). It establishes the legitimacy of the system, based on the provisional suspension of inequalities, and assumes access to the system and equal weight for everyone within that system. Paradoxically, the suspension of statutory inequalities in law (the same rights for all) coexists with the persistent inability of the legal system to properly moderate the disproportional capacities among the various categories of actors to assemble the resources required for legal disputes. Strategic lawsuits against public participation are only, when all is said and done, a politico-legal consequence of this failure. They are a symptom of a broader problem of recurrent legal inequality upon which SLAPPs rely.[13]

That, of course, does not mean that the actors with greater resources will inevitably be successful against their adversaries. This situation implies nevertheless that the actors (and categories of actors) who possess a sizeable legal capital — the capital of expertise and experience required for the conduct of a legal dispute — possess a considerable margin of maneuver permitting them to instrumentalize the economic inequalities between them and their adversaries in order to impose their will inside and outside the legal system. Legal intimidation operates on this principle: the threat of being dragged into a legal arena that is overly slow and costly by a very skilled team of legal experts (for months, and even years) leads competitors, political opponents and ordinary citizens to give into the demands of an adversary who knows it has an advantage.

SLAPPs are an epiphenomenon of a broader trend toward legal intimidation encouraged by a structural problem of accessibility to justice and legal inequality. Their specificity resides in the fact that they target citizens and groups mobilized around issues of public interest and that they therefore threaten the democratic vitality of a political community. Legal intimidation, whether or not it is political, has its foundations in persistent inequalities brought into the very core of the institution charged with remedying them. The elimination of these inequalities would put an end to SLAPPs as a distinct phenomenon of legal intimidation.

Simply through their existence, SLAPPs expose and challenge the myth of a liberal, egalitarian, equitable justice system that suspends inequalities of wealth and influence.

Mitigating the Symptoms

In the light of these reflections, it seems that the potential of the anti-SLAPP laws adopted in Quebec, considered in Canada and being implemented elsewhere in the world (in the United States in particular) is at best limited. The most relevant laws permit at once the effective protection of citizens from such lawsuits, compensation for SLAPP victims, dissuasion for those who might be tempted to use this practice of legal intimidation and severe punishment for those who use it. They therefore constitute real and significant protections against the abusive political instrumentalization of the failures and limitations of the liberal legal apparatus. Anti-SLAPP legislation, however, remains incapable of calling into question the logic that produced the phenomenon of legal intimidation that they are supposed to remedy. These laws offer superficial responses to failures of justice, and thus only serve to reaffirm the legitimacy of the legal institution in the face of the criticism of its detractors.

Such corrective measures will therefore not be able to deal satisfactorily with the underlying phenomenon, of which SLAPPs are ultimately only a symptom: a symptom of how economic influences have seeped into the legal system; of the increasing influence of the legal and judicial on political life, encouraging the judicialization of public debates and the reformulation of political conflicts into legal disputes; of a permanent colonization of the social world by the law and its instrumental logic. SLAPPs are a symptom, essentially, of an inordinate growth of the liberal justice system — and of the interests that it represents — to the detriment other modes of non-judicial conflict resolution.

The efforts deployed by the Quebec anti-SLAPP movement (and by others abroad) are part of a national and international movement for the reform of the justice system. There was never any question of challenging the structural factors that favour the emergence of SLAPPs or of demanding a radical rethink of the organization of justice. Reform was rather, in accordance with the state ideals of that justice system, a matter of favouring respect for freedom of expression considered as a fundamental right under attack by an illegitimate practice of judicial intimidation.

It is not, however, possible to heal an affliction with a remedy whose function is solely to mitigate the symptoms. At best, such a remedy permits us to live better with the ailment. The adoption of an anti-SLAPP law, as effective as it may be, can only mitigate the problems created by the growing influence of an inequitable justice system. In the absence of a coherent political will to name and then attack the factors that have favoured the emergence of abusive lawsuits, the best thing is to fight these legal actions.

This chapter, and this book as a whole, is based on a specific political ethics that may not be shared by all readers. A choice has been made here to give precedence to political rights and a principle of citizen participation in public debate over certain individual rights, including the right to reputation. This perspective involves a certain tolerance for faults, omissions, errors and inaccuracies that could be committed in good faith during public controversies. Finally, the argument in favour of rejecting the unwarranted judicialization of public debates requires that we put our faith in the intelligence of people and their ability to decide, by and for themselves, what they consider to be in the public interest.

The approach adopted here contrasts, ultimately, with the persistent blindness of the legal system to the processes of translating economic inequalities into legal inequalities, which favour the gagging of citizen expression. It will not please everyone and clashes with a principle of personal responsibility that encourages the legal punishment of faults and errors committed during public controversies — even when these faults are committed in good faith and when this participation is intended to be in the public interest. Critical readers who see this as an unproductive removal of individual responsibility will be able nevertheless to find in these pages arguments that will help them to promote legislative reforms that are limited to the proceedings of which the primary objective — and not the consequence — is to gag social and political opposition.

Notes

1. See, for example, Li (2009) on the concept of "rights consciousness."
2. This can be seen, for example, in the discourse around the "right to housing," the "right to a healthy environment" and the "right to development."
3. This role is moreover strongly contested by various Canadian authors. See Martin 2003; Leishman 2006.
4. The Supreme Court possesses three powers to remedy laws that contravene the Charter: invalidation, suspended declaration of constitutional invalidity and legislative amendment. To this is added the exclusive jurisdiction of the Supreme Court to determine the meaning given to rights and freedoms by the Charter and the assessment by the Court of the reasonable limits that can be placed on these rights in a free and democratic society. These powers influence the relationship between the legal and legislative branches of the government by partially subordinating the work of legislators (elected regulatory authorities accountable to the electorate) to that of judges (regulatory authorities who are appointed and irremovable). See Manfredi 2001: 195.
5. Anleu identifies in particular three categories of sanctions used by the state when legal norms are violated: they can be repressive/punitive (imprisonment being the prime example); restitutive (compensation for injured parties); or regulatory (the state can used its administrative apparatus against wrongdoers) (Anleu 2000: 139).

6. Forbidding English as a language of commercial signage was considered contrary to the principle of freedom of expression entrenched in the Canadian *Charter of Rights and Freedoms*. See *Ford c. Québec* (Procureur général), 2 R.C.S. 712, 1988.
7. *D.G.M.R., section locale 558 c. Pepsi-Cola Canada Beverages (West) Ltd.*, 1 R.C.S. 156, 2002 CSC 8.
8. Written transcripts, Bélanger, Michel, "Consultations particulières sur le projet de loi n° 99 — Loi modifiant le Code de procédure civile pour prévenir l'utilisation abusive des tribunaux et favoriser le respect de la liberté d'expression et la participation des citoyens aux débats publics," *Journal des débats*, 40, 63, Québec, Assemblée nationale du Québec, Commission des institutions, October 15, 2008; written transcripts, Lessard, Guy, "Consultations particulières sur le projet de loi n° 99 – Loi modifiant le Code de procédure civile pour prévenir l'utilisation abusive des tribunaux et favoriser le respect de la liberté d'expression et la participation des citoyens aux débats publics," *Journal des débats*, 40, 64, Québec, Assemblée nationale du Québec, Commission des institutions, October 22, 2008.
9. The Quebec Minister of Justice, Linda Goupil, pointed out in 1999 the "great disaffection of the Quebec population with the courts," declaring that "the costs, complexity and unwieldiness of proceedings have alienated people from the justice system" (quoted in Boucher 1999).
10. The judges appointed to the Supreme Court of Canada sit with security of tenure until the age of seventy-five. They can only be removed in exceptional cases and through a cumbersome procedure. This is supposed to ensure independence of the judiciary from political powers and prevent any unwarranted politicization of the Canadian legal system.
11. Serge Ménard, former Quebec Minister of Justice, declared, for example, that "accessibility of justice remains, in civil matters, the greatest problem that needs to be solved when we talk about justice" (1999).
12. Legal aid ensures minimum accessibility to justice for the most disadvantaged in Quebec society; the Fonds d'aide au recours collectif [aid fund for class action suits] is intended to permit ordinary citizens to oppose legally organizations and institutions that possess substantial legal capital. A very old, pious principle of charity is also expressed through the *pro bono* (unpaid) work done by many lawyers.
13. MNA Stéphane Bédard illustrated this phenomenon in very clear terms during the public hearings on SLAPPs that took place in the spring of 2008 in Quebec: "Faced with a multinational with unlimited means, even though we give every means to our justice system to be independent, the inequality of means remains real. When one party is able to hire 200 experts while the other party is unable to pay one, or even a lawyer, there is a real imbalance. So, what we are trying to do today is rebalance the forces, soon I hope, within the framework of a bill" (Bédard 2008).

Chapter 6

Conclusion

"Judicial procedure, they say, should not be the mistress, but the handmaiden of justice" (*Hamel c. Brunelle*, 1 R.C.S. 147, 156, 1977). Its task is to ensure sound, prompt and effective management of proceedings. It has to be applied to make the legal dispute a question of law, a debate on the attribution by the state of fault in concordance with the legislation in effect and jurisprudence, and not a matter of resources or power. In Quebec, it is considered to be a "privileged vehicle to assert substantive law before the courts" (Comité de révision de la procédure civile 2001). It has to therefore play a backstage role and not be overly apparent in the conflict that it regulates, tempers and administers.

This is a nice image that has very little to do with reality. Judicial procedure is not only that docile creature serving the sound functioning of the justice system. It is also a weapon, a pressure lever that is both powerful and effective. Judicial procedure is frightening; it drains significant resources and it feels like a maze to many. It is of such complexity that those who pride themselves in having navigated the legal system can demand, for their valuable services and their sage advice, huge fees.

Whatever the views of the judicial elites who might regret it, judicial procedure is actually the mistress — and an unfaithful one too — of substantive law. It sometimes favours the smooth resolution of conflicts and the emergence of equitable justice based on the law. At other times, it is diverted from these objectives, using its resources to avoid making decisions that contradict the interests of its current lovers. Judicial procedure is an instrument used by various categories of actors (individuals, lobby groups, corporations, public authorities and political figures, for example) who want to impose their will on adversaries in the public sphere or in the legal arena. This kind of legal action can lead to the financial exhaustion or psychological collapse of adversaries who possess less financial and legal capital. The use of legal proceedings is a question of choice, opportunism and strategy, as much as it is a question of justice.

The political instrumentalization of the judicial process constitutes an approach that is now very well established in North America. The extralegal advance of the law and of legal processes, along with the increasingly entrenched social and political reflex to make courts the arbitrators of the common good and public interest, help to fuel this trend. We should therefore not be surprised if certain self-serving interests take control of the judicial process and use it as a weapon of intimidation, censorship and repression; the context lends itself to this, and the legal system offers more powerful parties an arena in which they can drain the resources of their adversaries over long periods of time.

Therefore there is nothing astonishing about the emergence of SLAPPs as a phenomenon of legal intimidation. They are the product of persistent legal inequality and a strong tendency toward the instrumentalization of the rules related to legal disputes in order to obtain dominance on an issue being debated in the public sphere. They are the symptom of these phenomena and illustrate the increasing domestication of citizen communication power, the expression of a tendency toward the supervision and tight management of public debates through authoritarian legal norms that can be inhibiting.

In response, the anti-SLAPP struggle is being carried out on two distinct levels: concrete, on-the-ground resistance to attempts at legal muzzling, and pressure for legislative reform. The first level is defensive and privatizes the issues of the conflict: the fate of the victims is publicized and concern is expressed; support campaigns are organized; funds are raised in order to pay legal costs; legal proceedings instigated against citizen groups are denounced and deplored; the legal case is deconstructed and dissected. One looks for the flaws that will permit the court to show the action for what it is: the use of legal proceedings to deny or repress the exercise of rights that are supposed to be protected by the institution hearing the case. The second level is offensive and collectivizes the issues associated with the SLAPP: specific (often horrifying) cases are used to develop discourse on the need to make legislative reforms to discourage this practice and penalize those who use it. These actions are addressed respectively to the public and to the courts, or to the public and to lawmakers. In order to be effective, they require the development of a strong media presence identifying these legal actions as attempts at legal intimidation that are contrary to the fundamental values and principles of political participation and freedom of expression.

Whether defensive or offensive, these actions are essentially reformist: they usually do not call into question either the structural conditions that produced the SLAPP — and among other things, the organization of liberal justice on an inequitable capitalist model — nor do they question the legitimacy of the legal institution. Reform efforts fall short of disputing the logic of the legal institution and the language that it uses. So, for example, the concepts of the "diversion of the legal system" or the "diversion from the goals of the justice system," invoked emphatically by many stakeholders in Quebec and elsewhere in the world, are not usually analyzed critically within the framework of debates on the legal gagging of citizen expression.[1] Such critical analysis of the question of the diversion of the goals of the justice system requires that we reconsider the *very* nature of those goals: what are the interests served by the current organization of justice, by the substantial privatization of the costs associated with legal disputes, and by the free market of legal representation?

Discussions about SLAPPs therefore lend themselves to a broader reflection on the role of commercial relationships in the organization of the contemporary liberal justice system. This leads inevitably to a criticism of the political economy of justice. Seen from this perspective, strategic lawsuits against public participation constitute not an attempt at diversion of the supposedly primary goals of the legal system (to ensure the primacy of law, to make justice equitable and accessible), but the outcome of a logic supported by a system historically configured so as to ensure the reproduction of the interests of capital.[2] Current legal inequality exacerbates already significant social inequalities by dividing the litigants into two distinct categories: those who can easily afford the luxury of the legal representation of their personal interests and political positions, and those who can only through sometimes acute financial and psychological suffering assume the costs associated with legal disputes. The liberal justice system is the justice of economic liberalism. This is too often forgotten.

The jaws of legal proceedings are powerful weapons that can get a relentless hold on those being sued; they are not easy to escape for those being targeted. Simone de Beauvoir said that "a freedom which is interested only in denying freedom must be denied" (Beauvoir 1948: 91). The freedom to sue left and right should be denied in the name of a freedom of speech that needs protection, paradoxically by the law, from the legal actions intended to muzzle it.

The years I have spent studying the phenomenon and involving myself in the anti-SLAPP struggle have taught me respect and admiration for those who protect, against all odds, free citizen expression. These extraordinary men and women, armed with their convictions and inexhaustible energy, have provided us with an invaluable service. They have come under fire from all directions and devote huge amounts of time — which most of us spend on leisure activities — to invest their energy in public affairs, to reflect, to protest, to propose. They are the guardians of our democracy, the thorns that sometimes dig deep into the feet of those who complain when someone opposes their projects, ideas or interests. These people deserve substantial protection.

Not everyone shares the same analysis of the path taken in Quebec in recent years. Some see in the adoption of an anti-SLAPP law "a great victory" both personally and politically that has led to rulings exonerating them of any blame and legitimizing a principle of citizen participation in public debate.[3] Others optimistically consider that it will be "a solution that will permit the citizens of Quebec as well as citizen groups and organizations to participate in public debate and the protection of the environment without fear of being gagged and ruined by a gag suit."[4]

Some, finally, share an analysis very similar to the one I have developed in this book:

> The anti-SLAPP law will not be able to obscure this fundamental problem of the impossibility of full access to the courts for the vast majority of people. It is not on a very friendly basis that so many disputes are settled

"amicably," but on the basis of the impossibility of paying. Our justice system is not democratic. The anti-SLAPP law has even had the paradoxical effect of confirming, condoning and legitimizing this problem of access to justice to the extent that immunity is strictly for the groups that undergo the attacks of those who take advantage of the necessary services of highly paid lawyers to carry out their judicial operations. It is even said that, given that the legal system is highly unjust, given that it accepts at the centre of the process the economic concept of client (namely someone who has the means to take advantage of the services of a lawyer) rather than that of "citizen" (therefore someone who would have a de facto *right* to equitable representation), given that people can be forced into bankruptcy before they have even talked to a judge, given the demands of the process on the lives of people, we establish an anti-SLAPP law to protect certain social actors from the reality of these phenomena, so that they are not victims of certain abuses. The palliative nature of the law could not be expressed more clearly.[5]

Anti-SLAPP laws propose to mitigate the symptoms of a greater evil characterized by legal inequality and contamination of the social space by the law. They are all responses brought to the margins of a liberal justice system blind to its own deviations and biases. They therefore cannot — nor are they intended to — attack the root of the problem. Hence the important paradox that they create: these laws, by permitting us to better live with the dysfunctions of an institution essential in a democracy, both reaffirm principles of citizen participation in public debate and legitimize a system of justice that is organized to discourage it.

This paradox, as acute as it is, does not at all limit the relevance of legal and political demands requiring extensive protection for citizens involved in public debate against attempts at freedom-killing legal repression. The adoption of an anti-SLAPP law thus always represents a success, since it identifies an issue that could have been elusive and difficult to grasp for judicial and political authorities, who frequently show rather unproductive scepticism regarding the problem of SLAPPs. Simply having the legislation, however, is rarely enough; it has to have the teeth necessary to discourage legal gagging of social and political opposition. The citizens of Quebec have demonstrated admirable determination in acting "on a social question before it becomes a social problem" (Dupuis 2008). Nevertheless what needs to emerge is a more profound collective debate on the interests that are served by an institution exercising hegemonic power over the concept of "justice"; on the relationships of power and domination that this institution permits and reinforces; on the place occupied by the law, as a set of norms endorsed by the state, in the repression of the freedoms through which social criticism emerges and is practised. A rejection of censorship and silence is essential for the eventual emergence of this debate.

Notes

1. Professors Roderick A. Macdonald and Pierre Noreau, authors of the report on strategic lawsuits that serves as the basis for the legislative discussions on SLAPPs in Quebec, stated that the concept of the "diversion from the goals of the justice system" was "the most important standard" of their work, and they considered this question crucial for protecting the integrity of the legal system. Professor Noreau, for example, observed: "it is clear that we wanted to restore to judges the means to protect their own institution.... [The objective is] to give back to the judges the possibility of protecting their institution when they see that it is not being used for the purposes for which it was established, that is, to shed light on the law" (Macdonald and Noreau 2008).
2. This criticism has, for example, been formulated by authors belonging to the "*critical legal studies*" movement, established in the 1970s in the United States. For an overview of this approach, see, for example, Hutchinson 1999; Kelman 1987; Mangabeira Unger 1983.
3. This is in particular the view of Martin Drapeau, whose legal case was the first jurisprudence established on SLAPPs in Quebec (personal interview, March 2011).
4. Christine Landry, interviewed in March 2011.
5. Alain Deneault, interviewed in March 2011.

Appendices

Appendix 1: Bill 9

(2009, chapter 12)
An Act to amend the Code of Civil Procedure to prevent improper use of the courts and promote freedom of expression and citizen participation in public debate
Introduced 7 April 2009
Passed in principle 12 May 2009
Passed 3 June 2009
Assented to 4 June 2009
Québec Official Publisher
2009

EXPLANATORY NOTES
This Act amends the Code of Civil Procedure to promote freedom of expression and prevent improper use of the courts and the abuse of procedure, in particular if it thwarts the right of citizens to participate in public debate.

For that purpose, the Act allows the courts to promptly dismiss a proceeding that is improper. It specifies what may constitute an improper use of procedure and authorizes the reversal of the burden of proof if the improper use of procedure is summarily established. The Act also allows the courts to order the payment of a provision for costs, declare that a legal action is improper, condemn a party to pay the fees and extrajudicial costs of the other party, and order a party to pay punitive damages.

LEGISLATION AMENDED BY THIS ACT:
– Code of Civil Procedure (R.S.Q., chapter C-25).

Bill 9
AN ACT TO AMEND THE CODE OF CIVIL PROCEDURE TO PREVENT IMPROPER USE OF THE COURTS AND PROMOTE FREEDOM OF EXPRESSION AND CITIZEN PARTICIPATION IN PUBLIC DEBATE

AS it is important to promote freedom of expression affirmed in the Charter of human rights and freedoms;

AS it is important to prevent improper use of the courts and discourage judicial proceedings designed to thwart the right of citizens to participate in public debate;

AS it is important to promote access to justice for all citizens and to strike a fairer balance between the financial strength of the parties to a legal action;

THE PARLIAMENT OF QUÉBEC ENACTS AS FOLLOWS:

1. Article 26 of the Code of Civil Procedure (R.S.Q., chapter C-25) is amended by inserting the following subparagraph after subparagraph 4 of the second paragraph:

"(4.1) from any judgment that dismisses an action because of its improper nature;".

2. The Code is amended by inserting the following after article 54 in Chapter III of Title II of Book I concerning the powers of courts and judges:

"SECTION III

"POWER TO IMPOSE SANCTIONS FOR IMPROPER USE OF PROCEDURE

"54.1. A court may, at any time, on request or even on its own initiative after having heard the parties on the point, declare an action or other pleading improper and impose a sanction on the party concerned.

The procedural impropriety may consist in a claim or pleading that is clearly unfounded, frivolous or dilatory or in conduct that is vexatious or quarrelsome. It may also consist in bad faith, in a use of procedure that is excessive or unreasonable or causes prejudice to another person, or in an attempt to defeat the ends of justice, in particular if it restricts freedom of expression in public debate.

"54.2. If a party summarily establishes that an action or pleading may be an improper use of procedure, the onus is on the initiator of the action or pleading to show that it is not excessive or unreasonable and is justified in law. A motion to have an action in the first instance dismissed on the grounds of its improper nature is presented as a preliminary exception.

"54.3. If the court notes an improper use of procedure, it may dismiss the action or other pleading, strike out a submission or require that it be amended, terminate or refuse to allow an examination, or annul a writ of summons served on a witness.

In such a case or where there appears to have been an improper use of procedure, the court may, if it considers it appropriate,

(1) subject the furtherance of the action or the pleading to certain conditions;

(2) require undertakings from the party concerned with regard to the orderly conduct of the proceeding;

(3) suspend the proceeding for the period it determines;

(4) recommend to the chief judge or chief justice that special case management be ordered; or

(5) order the initiator of the action or pleading to pay to the other party, under pain of dismissal of the action or pleading, a provision for the costs of the proceeding, if justified by the circumstances and if the court notes that without such assistance the party's financial situation would prevent it from effectively arguing its case.

"54.4. On ruling on whether an action or pleading is improper, the court may order a provision for costs to be reimbursed, condemn a party to pay, in addition to costs, damages in reparation for the prejudice suffered by another party, including the fees and extrajudicial costs incurred by that party, and, if justified by the circumstances, award punitive damages.

If the amount of the damages is not admitted or may not be established easily at the time the action or pleading is declared improper, the court may summarily rule on the amount within the time and under the conditions determined by the court.

"54.5. If the improper use of procedure results from a party's quarrelsomeness, the court may, in addition, prohibit the party from instituting legal proceedings except with the authorization of and subject to the conditions determined by the chief judge or chief justice.

Appendix 2: British Columbia Bill (excerpts)

BILL 10 -- 2001 PROTECTION OF PUBLIC PARTICIPATION ACT
Definitions 1 (1) In this Act:
... "public participation" means communication or conduct aimed at influencing public opinion, or promoting or furthering lawful action by the public or by any government body, in relation to an issue of public interest, but does not include communication or conduct
(a) in respect of which an information has been laid or an indictment has been preferred in a prosecution conducted by the Attorney General or the Attorney General of Canada or in which the Attorney General or the Attorney General of Canada intervenes,
(b) that constitutes a breach of the *Human Rights Code* or any equivalent enactment of any other level of government,
(c) that contravenes any order of any court,
(d) that causes damage to or destruction of real property or personal property,
(e) that causes physical injury,
(f) that constitutes trespass to real or personal property, or
(g) that is otherwise considered by a court to be unlawful or an unwarranted interference by the defendant with the rights or property of a person;
"reasonable costs and expenses," in relation to a proceeding or claim, means costs and expenses that
(a) have been agreed on between the plaintiff and the defendant, or
(b) if no agreement has been reached, consist of the following:

    (i) the amount of legal fees and disbursements that are, in a review conducted under section 70 of the *Legal Profession Act* after the conclusion of the pro ceeding, determined to be owing by the defendant to the defendant's lawyers for all matters related to the proceeding or claim, as the case may be, including all of the reasonable costs and expenses incurred by the defendant in pursuing rights or remedies available under or contemplated by this Act in relation to the proceeding or claim, and for the purposes of the review under this subpa ragraph, the plaintiff is deemed to be, and to have standing to appear at the review as, a person charged within the meaning of the *Legal Profession Act*;

    (ii) any other costs and expenses that the registrar conducting the review considers to be reasonably incurred by the defendant in relation to the proceeding or claim.

(2) A proceeding or claim is brought or maintained for an improper purpose if
(a) the plaintiff could have no reasonable expectation that the proceeding or claim will succeed at trial, and
(b) a principal purpose for bringing the proceeding or claim is

    (i) to dissuade the defendant from engaging in public participation,

    (ii) to dissuade other persons from engaging in public participation,

(iii) to divert the defendant's resources from public participation to the proceeding, or

(iv) to penalize the defendant for engaging in public participation.

Purposes of this Act

2 The purposes of this Act are to

(a) encourage public participation, and dissuade persons from bringing or maintaining proceedings or claims for an improper purpose, by providing

(i) an opportunity, at or before the trial of a proceeding, for a defendant to allege that, and for the court to consider whether, the proceeding or a claim within the proceeding is brought or maintained for an improper purpose,

(ii) a means by which a proceeding or claim that is brought or maintained for an improper purpose can be summarily dismissed,

(iii) a means by which persons who are subjected to a proceeding or a claim that is brought or maintained for an improper purpose may obtain reimbursement for all reasonable costs and expenses that they incur as a result,

(iv) a means by which punitive or exemplary damages may be imposed in respect of a proceeding or claim that is brought or maintained for an improper purpose, and

(v) protection from liability for defamation if the defamatory communication or conduct constitutes public participation, and

(b) preserve the right of access to the courts for all proceedings and claims that are not brought or maintained for an improper purpose.

Defamation

3 Public participation constitutes an occasion of qualified privilege and, for that purpose, the communication or conduct that constitutes the public participation is deemed to be of interest to all persons who, directly or indirectly,

(a) receive the communication, or

(b) witness the conduct.

Application for summary dismissal

4 (1) If a defendant against whom a proceeding is brought or maintained considers that the whole of the proceeding or any claim within the proceeding has been brought or is being maintained for an improper purpose, the defendant may, subject to subsection (2), bring an application for one or more of the following orders:

(a) to dismiss the proceeding or claim, as the case may be;

(b) for reasonable costs and expenses;

(c) for punitive or exemplary damages against the plaintiff.

(2) If an application is brought under subsection (1),

(a) the applicant must set, as the date for the hearing of the application, a date that is

(i) not more than 60 days after the date on which the application is brought, and

(ii) not less than 120 days before the date scheduled for the trial of the proceeding, and

(b) all further applications, procedures or other steps in the proceeding are, unless the court otherwise orders, suspended until the application has been heard and decided.

(3) Nothing in subsection (2) (b) prevents the court from granting an injunction pending a determination of the rights under this Act of the parties to a proceeding.

Orders available to defendant

5 (1) On an application brought by a defendant under section 4 (1), the defendant may obtain an order under subsection (2) of this section if the defendant satisfies the court, on a balance of probabilities, that, when viewed on an objective basis,

(a) the communication or conduct in respect of which the proceeding or claim was brought constitutes public participation, and

(b) a principal purpose for which the proceeding or claim was brought or maintained is an improper purpose.

(2) If, on an application brought by a defendant under section 4 (1), the defendant satisfies the court under subsection (1) of this section in relation to the proceeding or in relation to a claim within the proceeding,

(a) the defendant may obtain one or both of the following orders:

(i) an order dismissing the proceeding or claim, as the case may be;

(ii) an order that the plaintiff pay all of the reasonable costs and expenses incurred by the defendant in relation to the proceeding or claim, as the case may be, including all of the reasonable costs and expenses incurred by the defendant in pursuing rights or remedies available under or contemplated by this Act in relation to the proceeding or claim, and

(b) the court may, in addition to the orders referred to in paragraph (a), on its own motion or on the application of the defendant, award punitive or exemplary damages against the plaintiff.

(3) If, on an application brought by a defendant under section 4 (1), the defendant is unable to satisfy the court under subsection (1) of this section, the defendant may obtain an order under subsection (4) if the defendant satisfies the court that there is a realistic possibility that, when viewed on an objective basis,

(a) the communication or conduct in respect of which the proceeding or claim was brought constitutes public participation, and

(b) a principal purpose for which the proceeding or claim was brought or maintained is an improper purpose.

(4) If, on an application brought by a defendant under section 4 (1), the defendant satisfies the court as required in subsection (3) of this section in relation to the proceeding or a claim within the proceeding, the court may make the following orders:

(a) an order, on the terms and conditions that the court considers appropriate, that

the plaintiff provide as security an amount that, in the court's opinion, will be sufficient to provide payment to the defendant of the full amounts of the reasonable costs and expenses and punitive or exemplary damages to which the defendant may become entitled under section 6;
(b) an order that any settlement, discontinuance or abandonment of the proceeding be effected with the approval of the court and on the terms the court considers appropriate.
(5) On an application for the settlement, discontinuance or abandonment of a proceeding or claim in respect of which an order was made under subsection (4), the court may, despite any agreement to the contrary between the defendant and the plaintiff, order the plaintiff to pay all of the reasonable costs and expenses incurred by the defendant in relation to the proceeding or claim, as the case may be, including all of the reasonable costs and expenses incurred by the defendant in pursuing rights or remedies available under or contemplated by this Act in relation to the proceeding or claim.
(6) If, in a proceeding in which the defendant has obtained an order under subsection (4), the defendant makes an application to dismiss the proceeding for want of prosecution, the defendant may obtain an order under subsection (7) of this section if
(a) the proceeding is dismissed for want of prosecution, and
(b) the plaintiff is unable to satisfy the court on the application that, when viewed on an objective basis,
  (i) the communication or conduct in respect of which the proceeding was brought does not constitute public participation, or
  (ii) none of the principal purposes for which the proceeding was brought or maintained were improper purposes.
(7) If, under subsection (6), the defendant is entitled to obtain an order under this subsection, the defendant may obtain an order that the plaintiff pay all of the reasonable costs and expenses incurred by the defendant in relation to the proceeding, including all of the reasonable costs and expenses incurred by the defendant in pursuing rights or remedies available under or contemplated by this Act in relation to the proceeding.

Onus on plaintiff at trial
6 (1) A defendant who has obtained an order under section 5 (4) in respect of a proceeding or claim may, at the trial of the proceeding, obtain one or more of the orders referred to in section 5 (2) if
(a) the defendant alleges at trial that
  (i) the communication or conduct in respect of which the proceeding or claim was brought constitutes public participation, and
  (ii) the proceeding or claim was brought or maintained for an improper purpose,

(b) the proceeding or claim is discontinued or abandoned by the plaintiff or is dismissed, and
(c) the plaintiff is unable to satisfy the court at trial that, when viewed on an objective basis,
    (i) the communication or conduct in respect of which the proceeding or claim was brought does not constitute public participation, or
    (ii) none of the principal purposes for which the proceeding or claim was brought or maintained were improper purposes.
(2) A defendant who has not obtained an order under section 5 (4) may, at the trial of the proceeding, obtain one or more of the orders referred to in section 5 (2) if
(a) the defendant gives notice to the plaintiff, at least 120 days before the date scheduled for the trial of the proceeding, that the defendant intends at trial to seek an order under this section in respect of a proceeding or claim,
(b) the defendant satisfies the court at trial that there is a realistic possibility that, when viewed on an objective basis,
    (i) the communication or conduct in respect of which the proceeding or claim was brought constitutes public participation, and
    (ii) a principal purpose for which the proceeding or claim was brought or maintained is an improper purpose,
(c) the proceeding or claim is discontinued or abandoned by the plaintiff or is dismissed, and
(d) the plaintiff is unable to satisfy the court at trial that, when viewed on an objective basis,
    (i) the communication or conduct in respect of which the proceeding or claim was brought does not constitute public participation, or
    (ii) none of the principal purposes for which the proceeding or claim was brought or maintained were improper purposes.

Court may hear any evidence and argument
7 (1) Without limiting any other rights the parties may have to present evidence and make arguments in an application brought under section 4 (1) or at a trial under section 6 (1) or (2), the parties may present evidence and make arguments as follows:
(a) as to whether the communication or conduct in relation to which the proceeding was brought constituted public participation;
(b) as to whether the proceeding was brought or is being maintained for an improper purpose.
(2) The parties may present the evidence or make the arguments referred to in subsection (1) (a) and (b) whether or not the evidence or arguments relate to the (1) (a) and (b) whether or not the evidence or arguments relate to the particulars of the claim or claims raised by the plaintiff.

Appendix 3: California Code of Civil Procedure

Sec. 425.16. Claim Arising from Person's Exercise of Constitutional Right of Petition or Free Speech -- Special Motion to Strike.
(a)   The Legislature finds and declares that there has been a disturbing increase in lawsuits brought primarily to chill the valid exercise of the constitutional rights of freedom of speech and petition for the redress of grievances. The Legislature finds and declares that it is in the public interest to encourage continued participation in matters of public significance, and that this participation should not be chilled through abuse of the judicial process. To this end, this section shall be construed broadly.
(b)   (1) A cause of action against a person arising from any act of that person in furtherance of the person's right of petition or free speech under the United States or California Constitution in connection with a public issue shall be subject to a special motion to strike, unless the court determines that the plaintiff has established that there is a probability that the plaintiff will prevail on the claim.

   (2)   In making its determination, the court shall consider the pleadings, and supporting and opposing affidavits stating the facts upon which the liability or defence is based.

   (3)   If the court determines that the plaintiff has established a probability that he or she will prevail on the claim, neither that determination nor the fact of that determination shall be admissible in evidence at any later stage of the case, or in any subsequent action, and no burden of proof or degree of proof otherwise applicable shall be affected by that determination in any later stage of the case or in any subsequent proceeding.
(c)   In any action subject to subdivision (b), a prevailing defendant on a special motion to strike shall be entitled to recover his or her attorney's fees and costs. If the court finds that a special motion to strike is frivolous or is solely intended to cause unnecessary delay, the court shall award costs and reasonable attorney's fees to a plaintiff prevailing on the motion, pursuant to Section 128.5.
(d)   This section shall not apply to any enforcement action brought in the name of the people of the State of California by the Attorney General, district attorney, or city attorney, acting as a public prosecutor.
(e)   As used in this section, "act in furtherance of a person's right of petition or free speech under the United States or California Constitution in connection with a public issue" includes:

   (1) any written or oral statement or writing made before a legislative, executive, or judicial proceeding, or any other official proceeding authorized by law;

   (2) any written or oral statement or writing made in connection with an issue under consideration or review by a legislative, executive, or judicial body, or any other official proceeding authorized by law;

   (3) any written or oral statement or writing made in a place open to the public

or a public forum in connection with an issue of public interest;

(4) or any other conduct in furtherance of the exercise of the constitutional right of petition or the constitutional right of free speech in connection with a public issue or an issue of public interest.

(f) The special motion may be filed within 60 days of the service of the complaint or, in the court's discretion, at any later time upon terms it deems proper. The motion shall be scheduled by the clerk of the court for a hearing not more than 30 days after the service of the motion unless the docket conditions of the court require a later hearing.

(g) All discovery proceedings in the action shall be stayed upon the filing of a notice of motion made pursuant to this section. The stay of discovery shall remain in effect until notice of entry of the order ruling on the motion. The court, on noticed motion and for good cause shown, may order that specified discovery be conducted notwithstanding this subdivision.

(h) For purposes of this section, "complaint" includes "cross-complaint" and "petition," "plaintiff" includes "cross-complainant" and "petitioner," and "defendant" includes "cross-defendant" and "respondent."

(i) An order granting or denying a special motion to strike shall be appealable under Section 904.1.

(j) (1) Any party who files a special motion to strike pursuant to this section, and any party who files an opposition to a special motion to strike, shall, promptly upon so filing, transmit to the Judicial Council, by e-mail or facsimile, a copy of the endorsed, filed caption page of the motion or opposition, a copy of any related notice of appeal or petition for a writ, and a conformed copy of any order issued pursuant to this section, including any order granting or denying a special motion to strike, discovery, or fees. (2) The Judicial Council shall maintain a public record of information transmitted pursuant to this subdivision for at least three years, and may store the information on microfilm or other appropriate electronic media.

LEGISLATIVE HISTORY: Added by Stats.1992, c. 726 (SB 1264), sec. 2. Amended by: Stats.1993, c. 1239 (SB 9), sec. 1, adding subd. (i) and substituting "shall" for "may" preceding "award costs" in subd. (c); Stats.1997, c. 271 (SB 1296), sec. 1, adding last sentence in subd. (a), adding subd. (e)(4), numbering subds. (e)(1)-(3), moving second sentence of subd. (g) to be second sentence of subd. (f), adding new subd. (h), and relettering former subd. (h) as subd. (i); and Stats.1999, c. 960 (AB 1675), sec. 1, adding subds. (j) and (k). Amended by Stats. 2005, c. 535 (AB 1158), amending subds. (b)(3), (f), deleting old subd. (i), relettering accordingly, and amending subd. (j)(1).

Uncodified legislative intent for amendment to subd. (f): "It is the intent of the Legislature, in amending subdivision (f) of Section 425.16 of the Code of Civil Procedure, to overrule the decisions in Decker v. U.D. Registry, Inc. (2003) 105 Cal.App.4th 1382, 1387-1390, and Fair Political Practices Commission v. American

Civil Rights Coalition, Inc. (2004) 121 Cal.App.4th 1171, 1174-1178." (Stats. 2005, c. 535, sec. 3.)

Section 425.17
(a) The Legislature finds and declares that there has been a disturbing abuse of Section 425.16, the California Anti-SLAPP Law, which has undermined the exercise of the constitutional rights of freedom of speech and petition for the redress of grievances, contrary to the purpose and intent of Section 425.16. The Legislature finds and declares that it is in the public interest to encourage continued participation in matters of public significance, and that this participation should not be chilled through abuse of the judicial process or Section 425.16.
(b) Section 425.16 does not apply to any action brought solely in the public interest or on behalf of the general public if all of the following conditions exist:
  (1) The plaintiff does not seek any relief greater than or different from the relief sought for the general public or a class of which the plaintiff is a member. A claim for attorney's fees, costs, or penalties does not constitute greater or different relief for purposes of this subdivision.
  (2) The action, if successful, would enforce an important right affecting the public interest, and would confer a significant benefit, whether pecuniary or nonpecuniary, on the general public or a large class of persons.
  (3) Private enforcement is necessary and places a disproportionate financial burden on the plaintiff in relation to the plaintiff's stake in the matter.
(c) Section 425.16 does not apply to any cause of action brought against a person primarily engaged in the business of selling or leasing goods or services, including, but not limited to, insurance, securities, or financial instruments, arising from any statement or conduct by that person if both of the following conditions exist:
  (1) The statement or conduct consists of representations of fact about that person's or a business competitor's business operations, goods, or services, that is made for the purpose of obtaining approval for, promoting, or securing sales or leases of, or commercial transactions in, the person's goods or services, or the statement or conduct was made in the course of delivering the person's goods or services.
  (2) The intended audience is an actual or potential buyer or customer, or a person likely to repeat the statement to, or otherwise influence, an actual or potential buyer or customer, or the statement or conduct arose out of or within the context of a regulatory approval process, proceeding, or investigation, except where the statement or conduct was made by a telephone corporation in the course of a proceeding before the California Public Utilities Commission and is the subject of a lawsuit brought by a competitor, notwithstanding that the conduct or statement concerns an important public issue.
(d) Subdivisions (b) and (c) do not apply to any of the following:
  (1) Any person enumerated in subdivision (b) of Section 2 of Article I of

the California Constitution or Section 1070 of the Evidence Code, or any person engaged in the dissemination of ideas or expression in any book or academic journal, while engaged in the gathering, receiving, or processing of information for communication to the public.

(2) Any action against any person or entity based upon the creation, dissemination, exhibition, advertisement, or other similar promotion of any dramatic, literary, musical, political, or artistic work, including, but not limited to, a motion picture or television program, or an article published in a newspaper or magazine of general circulation.

(3) Any nonprofit organization that receives more than 50 percent of its annual revenues from federal, state, or local government grants, awards, programs, or reimbursements for services rendered.

(e) If any trial court denies a special motion to strike on the grounds that the action or cause of action is exempt pursuant to this section, the appeal provisions in subdivision (j) of Section 425.16 and paragraph (13) of subdivision (a) of Section 904.1 do not apply to that action or cause of action.

LEGISLATIVE HISTORY: Added by Stats. 2003, c. 338 (SB 515).
Sec. 425.18. SLAPPbacks.
(Effective October 5, 2005)
425.18. (a) The Legislature finds and declares that a SLAPPback is distinguishable in character and origin from the ordinary malicious prosecution action. The Legislature further finds and declares that a SLAPPback cause of action should be treated differently, as provided in this section, from an ordinary malicious prosecution action because a SLAPPback is consistent with the Legislature's intent to protect the valid exercise of the constitutional rights of free speech and petition by its deterrent effect on SLAPP (strategic lawsuit against public participation) litigation and by its restoration of public confidence in participatory democracy.

(b) For purposes of this section, the following terms have the following meanings:

(1) "SLAPPback" means any cause of action for malicious prosecution or abuse of process arising from the filing or maintenance of a prior cause of action that has been dismissed pursuant to a special motion to strike under Section 425.16.

(2) "Special motion to strike" means a motion made pursuant to Section 425.16.

(c) The provisions of subdivisions (c), (f), (g), and (i) of Section 425.16, and paragraph (13) of subdivision (a) of Section 904.1, shall not apply to a special motion to strike a SLAPPback.

(d) (1) A special motion to strike a SLAPPback shall be filed within any one of the following periods of time, as follows:

(A) Within 120 days of the service of the complaint.

(B) At the court's discretion, within six months of the service of the complaint.

(C) At the court's discretion, at any later time in extraordinary cases due to no fault of the defendant and upon written findings of the court stating the extraordinary case and circumstance.

(d) (2) The motion shall be scheduled by the clerk of the court for a hearing not more than 30 days after the service of the motion unless the docket conditions of the court require a later hearing.

(e) A party opposing a special motion to strike a SLAPPback may file an ex parte application for a continuance to obtain necessary discovery. If it appears that facts essential to justify opposition to that motion may exist, but cannot then be presented, the court shall grant a reasonable continuance to permit the party to obtain affidavits or conduct discovery or may make any other order as may be just.

(f) If the court finds that a special motion to strike a SLAPPback is frivolous or solely intended to cause unnecessary delay, the court shall award costs and reasonable attorney's fees to a plaintiff prevailing on the motion, pursuant to Section 128.5.

(g) Upon entry of an order denying a special motion to strike a SLAPPback claim, or granting the special motion to strike as to some but less than all causes of action alleged in a complaint containing a SLAPPback claim, an aggrieved party may, within 20 days after service of a written notice of the entry of the order, petition an appropriate reviewing court for a peremptory writ.

(h) A special motion to strike may not be filed against a SLAPPback by a party whose filing or maintenance of the prior cause of action from which the SLAPPback arises was illegal as a matter of law.

(i) This section does not apply to a SLAPPback filed by a public entity.

LEGISLATIVE HISTORY: Added by Stats. 2005, c. 535 (AB 1158 — Lieber).

Bibliography

Abell, David J. 1993. "Comment: Exercise of Constitutional Privileges: Deterring Abuse of the First Amendment — Strategic Lawsuits Against Political Participation." *Southern Methodist University Law Review* 47: 95–130.

Abrams, Robert. 1989. "Strategic Lawsuits Against Public Participation (SLAPPs)." *Pace University Law Review* 7, 1: 33–44.

Agence QMI. 2011, February 28. "Marc Bellemare abandonne." *Droit Inc.com*.

Anleu, Sharyn L. Roach. 2000. *Law and Social Change*. London & Thousand Oaks, CA: Sage Publications.

Assemblée nationale du Québec. 2008, February 20. "Consultation générale sur les documents intitulés Rapport d'évaluation de la Loi portant réforme du Code de procédure civile et Les poursuites stratégiques contre la mobilisation publique — les poursuites-bâillons (SLAPP)." *Journal des débats*, 40, 27. Québec, Assemblée nationale du Québec, Commission des institutions.

Association québécoise de lutte contre la pollution atmosphérique and Comité de restauration de la rivière Etchemin (AQLPA and CREE). 2008, February 1. *Protéger le droit de participation du public: mémoire*, Québec, Assemblée nationale du Québec, Commission des institutions.

____. 2008. *Protéger le droit de participation du public : mémoire*. Québec, Assemblée nationale du Québec, Commission des institutions.

ATTAC-Québec. 2008. *Mémoire sur les poursuites stratégiques contre la mobilisation publique (SLAPP)*. Québec, Assemblée nationale du Québec, Commission des institutions.

Barker, John C. 1993. "Common-Law and Statutory Solutions to the Problem of SLAPPs." *Loyola of Los Angeles Law Review* 26, 2: 395–454.

____. (2004). "Chapter 338: Another New Law, Another SLAPP in the Face of California Business." *McGeorge Law Review* 35: 409–32.

Baruch, Chad. 1996. "If I Had a Hammer: Defending Slapp Suits in Texas." *Texas Wesleyan Law Review* 3: 55–70.

Beatty, Joseph W. 1997. "The Legal Literature on SLAPPs: A Look Behind the Smoke Nine Years After Professors Pring and Canan First Yelled 'Fire!'" *University of Florida Journal of Law & Public Policy* 9: 85–110.

Beauvoir, Simone de. 1948. *The Ethics of Ambiguity*. Translated by Bernard Frechtman. New York: Philosophical Library.

Bédard, Stéphane. 2008. "Consultation générale sur les documents intitulés Rapport d'évaluation de la Loi portant réforme du Code de procédure civile et Les poursuites stratégiques contre la mobilisation publique — les poursuites-bâillons (SLAPP)." *Journal des débats* 40, 34. Québec, Assemblée nationale du Québec, Commission des institutions.

Bédard, Stéphane, and Stéphane Tremblay. 2006, September 15. "Poursuite stratégique contre la mobilisation publique (SLAPP) — l'opposition officielle réclame à nouveau l'intervention du gouvernement du Québec." CNW *Telbec*.

Boivin, Simon. 2010, September 2. "Marc Bellemare poursuit Jean Charest à son tour." *Le Soleil*,

Bombardier, David. 2006, May 17. "Ferti-Val intente une poursuite de 700 000 $." *La*

Tribune, p. 13.

____. 2006, December 15a. "Sébastien Lussier 'énormément soulagé.'" *La Tribune*, p. 5.

____. 2006, December 15b. "Ferti-Val plaide coupable de nuisance." *La Tribune*, p. 5.

Boucher, Guylaine. 1999. "Allocution d'ouverture de la ministre Linda Goupil au congrès 1999: redonner confiance à la population." *Le Journal du Barreau* 31, 12. <http://www.barreau.qc.ca/publications/journal/vol31/no12/allocution.html>.

Bourgault-Côté, Guillaume. 2006, August 18. "Bâillon sur un groupe écolo." *Le Devoir*, p. A1.

____. 2006, October 11. "Une loi est demandée." *Le Devoir*, p. A5.

____. 2007, July 25. "Poursuites-bâillons: sale affaire en Outaouais," *Le Devoir*.

Bover, Travis, and Mark Parnell. 2001. *A Protection of Public Participation Act for South Australia: A Law Reform Proposal prepared for the Environmental Defenders Office (SA) Inc*. <http://www.edo.org.au/edosa/research/public %20participation.htm>.

Braun, Jerome I. 1999. "Increasing SLAPP Protection: Unburdening the Right of Petition in California." *U.C. Davis Law Review* 32: 969–70.

____. 2003. "California's Anti-SLAPP Remedy After Eleven Years." *McGeorge Law Review* 34, 4: 731–83.

Breton, Brigitte. 2006, September 26. "Défense ou intimidation." *Le Soleil*, p. 20.

Canan, Penelope. 1989. "SLAPPs from a Sociological Perspective." *Pace University Environmental Law Review* 7, 1: 23–32.

Canan, Penelope, and George W. Pring. 1988. "Studying Strategic Lawsuits Against Public Participation: Mixing Quantitative and Qualitative Approaches." *Law & Society Review* 22, 2: 385–95.

Clément, Dominique. 2008. *Canada's Rights Revolution: Social Movements and Social Change, 1937–82*. Vancouver: UBC Press.

Cloutier, Christophe. 2011, October 19. "Goliath a gagné!" *Le Devoir*.

Cohen, Mark A. 2010, July 23. "Anti-SLAPP law decision overturned by Minnesota Court of Appeals." *AllBusiness.com*.

Comité de révision de la procédure civile. 2001. *La révision de la procédure civile*. Québec, Bibliothèque nationale du Québec. <www.justice.gouv.qc.ca/francais/publications/rapports/pdf/crpc/crpc-rap1-intro.pdf>.

Confédération des syndicats nationaux. 2008. *Mémoire présenté par la Confédération des syndicats nationaux à la Commission des institutions sur la réforme du Code de procédure civile et les poursuites stratégiques contre la mobilisation publique*. Québec, Assemblée nationale du Québec, Commission des institutions.

Conseil du patronat du Québec. 2008. *Pour un équilibre des droits: mémoire du Conseil du patronat du Québec sur le projet de loi 99, Loi modifiant le Code de procédure civile pour prévenir l'utilisation abusive des tribunaux et favoriser le respect de la liberté d'expression et la participation des citoyens aux débats publics*. Québec, Assemblée nationale du Québec, Commission des institutions.

Costantini, Edmond, and Mary Paul Nash. 1991. "SLAPP/SLAPPback: The Misuse of Libel Law for Political Purposes and a Countersuit Response." *The Journal of Law & Politics* 7, 3: 417–79.

Corby, Dora A. 1998. "Clearing Up Civil Procedure Section 425.16 — Delivering the Final Knockout Punch to SLAPP Suits." *McGeorge Law Review* 29: 469–67.

Dickner, Nicolas. 2011, November 2. "Restez à l'écoute." *Voir.ca*.

Donson, Fiona J. L. 2000. *Legal Intimidation: A Slapp in the Face of Democracy*. London: Free Association Books.

Duplessis, Marie-Pier. 2013, June 17. "Congédiement de Jean-François Jacob: commentaires négatifs envers Desjardins." *Le Soleil.*

Dupuis, Jacques. 2008. "Consultation générale sur les documents intitulés Rapport d'évaluation de la Loi portant réforme du Code de procédure civile et Les poursuites stratégiques contre la mobilisation publique — les poursuites-bâillons (SLAPP)." *Journal des débats* 40, 39. Québec, Assemblée nationale du Québec, Commission des institutions.

Écosociété. 2008. *Attaque à la liberté d'expression: Écosociété est l'objet de deux SLAPP.* <slapp.ecosociete.org/fr/node/65>.

Ericson-Siegel, Laura J. 1992. "Silencing SLAPPs: An Examination of Proposed Legislative Remedies and a 'Solution' for Florida." *Florida State University Law Review* 20, 2: 487–516.

Fédération des chambres de commerce du Québec. 2008. *Mémoire présenté à la Commission des institutions dans le cadre des consultations publiques à l'égard du projet de loi no 99, Loi modifiant le Code de procédure civile pour prévenir l'utilisation abusive des tribunaux et favoriser le respect de la liberté d'expression et la participation des citoyens aux débats publics.* Québec, Assemblée nationale du Québec, Commission des institutions.

Fédération professionnelle des journalistes du Québec. 2011, February 22. "Le maire Labeaume n'a pas à menacer les médias." FPJQ.

Foucault, Michel. 1975. *Surveiller et punir: naissance de la prison.* Paris: Gallimard.

Furman, Joshua R. 2001. "Cybersmear or Cyber-SLAPP: Analyzing Defamation Suits Against Online John Does as Strategic Lawsuits Against Public Participation." *Seattle University Law Review* 25: 213–54.

Galipeau, Serge. 2008. "Consultation générale sur les documents intitulés Rapport d'évaluation de la Loi portant réforme du Code de procédure civile et Les poursuites stratégiques contre la mobilisation publique — les poursuites-bâillons (SLAPP)." *Journal des débats* 40, 27. Québec, Assemblée nationale du Québec, Commission des institutions.

Glaetzer, Sally. 2010, January 30. "Gunns 20 in the dust." themercury.com. <www.themercury.com.au/arti-cle/2010/01/30/124821_todays-news.html>.

Goetz, Stacy. 1992. "SLAPP Suits: A Problem for Public Interest Advocates and Connecticut Courts." *Bridgeport Law Review* 12: 1005–34.

Gray, Jeff. 2007, May 3. "Port Authority's cynical SLAPP aimed at silencing its critics." *Globe and Mail,* p. A13.

Groupe de travail sur la révision du régime d'aide juridique au Québec. 2005. *Pour une plus grande accessibilité à la justice: rapport du Groupe de travail sur la révision du régime d'aide juridique au Québec.* Québec, Ministère de la Justice du Québec.

Habermas, Jürgen. 1984. *The Theory of Communicative Action v. 2: Lifeworld and System: A Critique of Functionalist Reason.* Boston: Beacon Press.

___. 1992. "Further Reflections on the Public Sphere." In Craig Calhoun (ed.), *Habermas and the Public Sphere.* Cambridge: MIT Press.

___. 1996. *Between Facts and Norms: Contributions to a Discourse Theory of Law and Democracy.* Cambridge: MIT Press.

Huling, Geoffrey Paul. 1994. "Tired of Being Slapped Around: States Take Action Against Lawsuits Designed to Intimidate and Harass." *Rutgers Law Journal* 25, 2: 401–32.

Hutchinson, Allan C. (ed.). 1999. *Critical Legal Studies.* Totowa, NJ: Rowman & Littlefield.

Ignatieff, Michael. 2000. *The Rights Revolution.* Toronto: House of Anansi Press.

Jackson, D. Mark. 2001. "The Corporate Defamation Plaintiff in the Era of SLAPPs: Revisiting *New York Times* v. Sullivan." *William & Mary Bill of Rights Journal* 9, 2: 491–523.
Jarry, Monique. 2005. *Une petite histoire de l'aide juridique*. <www.csj.qc.ca/SiteComm/W2007English/.\Pdf/historique.pdf>.
Kelman, Mark. 1987. *A Guide to Critical Legal Studies*. Cambridge: Harvard University Press.
Knopff, Rainer, and Frederick Lee Morton. 1992. *Charter Politics*. Scarborough: Nelson.
Kohler, David. 2004. "Forty Years after *New York Times* v. Sullivan: The Good, the Bad, and the Ugly." *Oregon Law Review* 83, 4: 1203–38.
La Tribune. 2006, April 29. "Les voisins de Ferti-Val déposent une pétition demandant la fermeture de l'entreprise."
Lalonde, Michelle. 2011, June 6. "Lawsuits are muting public protest. Lawsuits designed to intimidate and silence critics are illegal in Quebec, but they haven't stopped — and can cost activists dearly." *Montreal Gazette*.
Landry, Normand. 2010. "From the Streets to the Courtroom: The Legacies of Quebec's anti-SLAPP Movement." *Review of European Community and International Environmental Law* 19, 1: 58–69.
Leishman, Rory. 2006. *Against Judicial Activism: The Decline of Freedom and Democracy in Canada*. Montreal: McGill-Queen's University Press.
Lemonde, Lucie, and Gabrielle Ferland-Gagnon. 2010. "Les étapes de la mobilisation citoyenne et de l'adoption de la loi contre les poursuites-bâillons." *Les Cahiers de droit*, 51: 95–221.
Li, Lianjiang. 2009, August 20. *Rights Consciousness and Rules Consciousness in Contemporary China*. Toronto: Annual Meeting of the American Political Science Association. <http://ssrn.com/abstract=1458223>.
Ligue des droits et libertés. 2008. *Pour une protection efficace des victimes de poursuites-bâillons: Brief presented to the Committee on Institutions on Bill 99: An Act to amend the Code of Civil Procedure to prevent improper use of the courts and promote freedom of expression and citizen participation in public debate*. Quebec City: National Assembly of Quebec, Committee on Institutions.
____. 2009, March 5. "Loi anti-bâillon: une adoption avant juin 2009 est réclamée!" *Ligue des droits et libertés*. <www.liguedes droits.ca/publications/communiques/loi-anti-baillon-une-adoption-avant-juin-2009-est-reclamee.html>.
Lott, Susan. 2004. *Corporate Retaliation Against Consumers: The Status of Strategic Lawsuits Against Public Participation (SLAPPs) in Canada*. Ottawa: Public Interest Advocacy Centre. <www.piac.ca/files/slapps.pdf>.
Lussier, Sébastien. 2008. Interview with Julien Fréchette. *SLAPP 101*. Parole citoyenne. <parolecitoyenne.org/slapp-101?dossier_nid=23194>.
MacDonald, Roderick A., Daniel Jutras and Pierre Noreau. 2007. *Les poursuites stratégiques contre la mobilisation publique — les poursuites-bâillons (SLAPP)*. Québec, Ministère de la Justice du Québec. <www.justice.gouv.qc.ca/Francais/publications/rapports/pdf/slapp.pdf>.
Macdonald, Roderick A., and Pierre Noreau. 2008. "Consultations particulières sur le projet de loi n° 99 — Loi modifiant le Code de procédure civile pour prévenir l'utilisation abusive des tribunaux et favoriser le respect de la liberté d'expression et la participation des citoyens aux débats publics." *Journal des débats* 40, 63. Québec, Assemblée nationale du Québec, Commission des institutions.
Manfredi, Christopher P. 2001. *Judicial Power and the Charter: Canada and the Paradox of*

Liberal Constitutionalism. 2nd edition. Don Mills: Oxford University Press.
Mangabeira Unger, Roberto. 1983. *The Critical Legal Studies Movement.* Cambridge: Harvard University Press.
Margonty, Luce. 2006, September 14. "Mobilisation contre les poursuites stratégiques." *La Presse,* p. A5.
Martin, Robert Ivan. 2003. *The Most Dangerous Branch.* Montreal: McGill-Queen's University Press.
Mazeaud, Jean, Henry Mazeaud and Léon Mazeaud. 1972. *Leçons de droit civil.* Volume one. 5th edition. Paris: Montchrestie.
McBride, Edward W. Jr. 1993. "The Empire State SLAPPs Back: New York's Legislative Response to SLAPP Suits." *Vermont Law Review* 17, 3: 925–58.
McCann, Michael W. 1994. *Rights at Work: Pay Equity Reform and the Politics of Legal Mobilization.* Chicago: University of Chicago Press.
McCarthy, Carlotta E. 1998. "Constitutional Law — Citizens Cannot Be 'SLAPPed' for Exercising First Amendment Right to Petition the Government — Hometown Properties, Inc. v. Fleming, 680 A.2d 56 (R.I. 1996)." *Suffolk University Law Review.*
McEvoy, Sharlene A. 1990. "'The Big Chill': Business Use of the Tort of Defamation to Discourage the Exercise of First Amendment Rights." *Hastings Constitutional Law Quarterly* 17: 503–32.
McLachlin, Beverley. 2009. "Courts, Legislatures and Executives in the Post-Charter Era." In Paul Howe and Peter H. Russell (eds.), *Judicial Power and Canadian Democracy.* Montreal: McGill-Queen's University Press.
Ménard, Serge. 1999. *Le Journal du Barreau* 31, 1. <www.barreau.qc.ca/publications/journal/vol31/no1/accessibilite.html>.
Merry, Sally Engle. 1990. *Getting Justice and Getting Even: Legal Consciousness Among Working-Class Americans.* Chicago: University of Chicago Press.
Monton, Frederick L. 2002. *Law, Politics and the Judicial Process in Canada.* Calgary: University of Calgary Press.
Moran, Mayo, Brian MacLeod Rogers and Peter Downard. 2010, October 28. *Anti-SLAPP Advisory Panel: Report to the Attorney General.* <www.attorneygeneral.jus.gov.on.ca/english/anti_slapp/anti_slapp_final_report_en. pdf>.
Noreau, Pierre. 2005. Interview with Julien Fréchette "SLAPP 101." *Office national du film du Canada.* <parole citoyenne.org/slapp-101>.
Ogle, Greg. 2005. *Gunning for Change: The Need for Public Participation Law Reform.* Hobart: The Wilderness Society Inc. <users.senet.com.au/~gregogle/images/Gunning_for_Change_web.pdf>.
Parent, Olivier. 2013, May 25."Victime d'une 'poursuite bâillon,' par CHOI Radio X." *La Presse.*
Pelletier, Vincent. 2008. "Strategic Lawsuits against Public Participation (SLAPPs) (and other abusive lawsuits)." Proceedings of the Uniform Law Conference of Canada.
Perell, Paul. 2007. "A Survey of Abuse of Process." In Todd L. Archibald and Randall Scott Echlin (eds.), *Annual Review of Civil Litigation.* Toronto: Carswell.
Pring, George W. 1989. "SLAPPs: Strategic Lawsuits Against Public Participation." *Pace University Environmental Law Review* 7, 1: 3–22.
Pring, George W., and Penelope Canan. 1996. *SLAPPs: Getting Sued for Speaking Out.* Philadelphia: Temple University Press.
Protégez-vous. 2009. "Guide pratique de l'accès à la justice."

Quebec. 2009. *An Act to amend the Code of Civil Procedure to prevent improper use of the courts and promote freedom of expression and citizen participation in public debate.* <http://www2.publicationsduquebec.gouv.qc.ca/dynamicSearch/telecharge.php?type=5&file=2009C12A.PDF>.

Quebec Bar. 2008. *Consultations particulières et audiences publiques à l'égard du projet de loi no 99, Loi modifiant le Code de procédure civile pour prévenir l'utilisation abusive des tribunaux et favoriser le respect de la liberté d'expression et la participation des citoyens aux débats publics.* Québec, Assemblée nationale du Québec, Commission des institutions.

Rickarby, Liesel. 2010, January 28. "Gunns 20 Case Goes to Trial." *newmathilda.com.* <http://newmatilda.com/2010/01/28/gunns20-goes-to-trial>.

Robitaille, Antoine. 2010, September 9. "Marc Bellemare poursuit Jean Charest pour 900 000 $." *Le Devoir.*

Rowell, Andrew. 1998. "SLAPPing Resistance." *The Ecologist* 28, 5: 302–303.

Russell, Peter H. 1982. "The Effect of a Charter of Rights on the Policy-Making Role of Canadian Courts." *Canadian Public Administration* 25, 1: 1–33.

Sankoff, Peter. 2004. "The Application of Section 24(2) of the Charter of Rights and Freedoms in a Civil Action." *Advocates Quarterly* 28: 103–31

Santerre, David. 2008, June 16. "Faire taire les citoyens." *Journal de Montréal.*

Scott, Michaelin, and Chris Tollefson. 2010. "Strategic Lawsuits Against Public Participation: The British Columbia Experience." *Review of European Community & International Environmental Law* 19, 1: 45–57.

Shapiro, Pamela. 2010. "SLAPPs: Intent or Content? Anti-SLAPP Legislation Goes International." *Review of European Community & International Environmental Law* 19, 1: 14–27.

Shields, Alexandre. 2009, March 6. "Le projet de loi contre les SLAPP revivra. Plusieurs organismes demandent à la ministre de la Justice d'agir rapidement." *Le Devoir.*

____. 2013, April 26. "Écosociété règle hors cour son litige avec la minière Banro." *Le Devoir.*

Sills, Jennifer E. 1993. "SLAPPs (Strategic Lawsuits Against Public Participation): How Can the Legal System Eliminate Their Appeal?" *Connecticut Law Review* 25, 2: 547–83.

Silverstein, Gordon. 2009. *Law's Allure: How Law Shapes, Constrains, Saves, and Kills Politics.* Cambridge & New York: Cambridge University Press.

Smith, Rick. 2008, February 26. "Democracy suffers under barrage of strategic lawsuits." <http://www.thestar.com/opinion/2008/02/26/democracy_suffers_under_barrage_of_strategic_lawsuits.html>.

Société Radio-Canada. 2006, September 21. "Québec ferme le dépotoir de Cantley." Radio-Canada.ca.

____. 2006, October 3. "Faire taire les citoyens à n'importe quel prix?" Radio-canada.ca.

____. 2006, December 20. "Forte amende pour Ferti-Val." Radio-Canada.ca.

____. 2008, February 18. "On les appelle les poursuites abusives. Elles surviennent quand une partie utilise les tribunaux pour intimider et faire taire toute forme d'opposition." *Le Point.*

____. 2008, May 6. "Poursuite-bâillon en vue." Radio-Canada.ca.

____. 2011, February 23. "La FPJQ demande à Régis Labeaume de retirer ses menaces de poursuite." *Radio-Canada.ca.*

____. 2011, August 24. "Bataille judiciaire entre la SRC et Constructions Louisbourg." Radio-Canada.ca.

Stein, Michael. 1989. "SLAPP Suits: A Slap at the First Amendment." *Pace University*

Environmental Law Review 7: 45–59.

Stetson, Marnie. 1995. "Reforming SLAPP Reform: New York's Anti-SLAPP Statute." *New York University Law Review* 70: 1324–61.

Teubner, Gunther (ed.). 1987. *Juridification of Social Spheres: A Comparative Analysis in the Areas of Labor, Corporate, Antitrust & Social Welfare Law*. Berlin & New York: De Gruyter.

Thériault, Charles. 2011, February 21. "L'héritage d'un long combat judiciaire." *Le Droit,*

____. 2011, May 7. "Le couple Landry-Galipeau déçu de leur dédommagement." *Le Droit.*

Tocqueville, Alexis de. 2010. *Democracy in America: Historical-Critical Edition of De la démocratie en Amérique*. Edited by Eduardo Nolla. Translated by James T. Schleifer. Volume 2. Indianapolis: Liberty Fund.

Tollefson, Chris. 1994. "Strategic Lawsuits Against Public Participation: Developing a Canadian Response." *Canadian Bar Review* 73, 2: 200–33.

____. 1996. "Strategic Lawsuits and Environmental Politics: Daishowa Inc. v. Friends of the Lubicon." *Journal of Canadian Studies* 31, 1: 1–19.

Trudel, Pierre. 2001. *Droit de l'information et de la communication*. DRT 3805. Montréal: Université de Montréal, Faculté de droit.

____. 2007, July 19. "Les poursuites-baîllons et le droit à la réputation." *Le Devoir.*

Vick, Douglas W., and Kevin Campbell. 2001. "Public Protests, Private Lawsuits, and the Market: The Investor Response to the McLibel Case." *Journal of Law and Society* 28, 2: 204–41.

Waldman, Thomas A. 1993. "SLAPP Suits: Weaknesses in First Amendment Law and in the Courts' Responses to Frivolous Litigation." UCLA *Law Review* 39: 979–1053.

Walters, Brian. 2003. *Slapping on the Writs: Defamation, Developers and Community Activism*. Sidney: University of New South Wales Press.

Weir, Elizabeth. 2004. "SLAPping the Citizenry. Public Criticism of a Corporation Can Land You in Court." Rabble.ca. <http://rabble.ca/news/slapping-citizenry>.

Wells, James A. 1998. "Exporting SLAPPs: International Use of the U.S. "SLAPP" to Suppress Dissent and Critical Speech." *Temporary International and Comparative Law* 12, 2: 457–502.